An Abridged History of World Religions

An Abridged History of World Religions

Rex A. Lentz

Writer's Showcase
San Jose New York Lincoln Shanghai

An Abridged History of World Religions

All Rights Reserved © 2002 by Rex A. Lentz

No part of this book may be reproduced or transmitted in any form or by any means, graphic, electronic, or mechanical, including photocopying, recording, taping, or by any information storage retrieval system, without the permission in writing from the publisher.

Writer's Showcase
an imprint of iUniverse, Inc.

For information address:
iUniverse, Inc.
5220 S. 16th St., Suite 200
Lincoln, NE 68512
www.iuniverse.com

ISBN: 0-595-23062-8

Printed in the United States of America

To Violet

Contents

Introduction xi

CHAPTER 1 BCE 1
Before the Common Era

CHAPTER 2 0–300 CE 21
The Early Christians

CHAPTER 3 300–600 CE 37
Constantine through Augustine

CHAPTER 4 500–900 CE 51
Islam

CHAPTER 5 700–800 CE 61
Charlemagne

CHAPTER 6 1096–1270 (1492) 67
Crusades

CHAPTER 7 1500–1600 CE 77
Reformation

CHAPTER 8 1600–To Date 91
Getting Organized

CHAPTER 9 1800–To Date 113
Modern History Of Denominations

CHAPTER 10 To Date 159
A Changing World

APPENDIX   World Religion Tree...................... 163
Bibliography.. 165
Index 169

Acknowledgements

Violet, my wife, whose encouragement and editing kept my book going to completion.

Tim Lentz PhD, my number two son, whose literary counsel was greatly appreciated.

Diana Lentz, my daughter-in-law, and my computer end user support who always had the correct solution. Her dedicated efforts in formatting this text, completing the corrections and making sure all was in order are deeply appreciated.

Introduction

Having reached the age of eighty-two years I felt compelled to leave my children and grandchildren a broad, if brief, understanding of the world religions as I see them. I am not a theological analyst but I can approach the subject of religion historically. Yesterday's heretic may have a philosophy that could be a main line church today. As archaeologists dig, scholars study and historians search, it reveals an ever-changing religious structure. The distrust and even hatred between churches that caused so many wars may be easing but has not ended, perhaps it never will. Understanding through knowledge and love is the only answer. It is most important then to first look at the history of religion and gain knowledge as to why, when, and how we created such diversity and distrust. The answer is described in the pages of history. I am not suggesting I can do this better than the fifty books on religion that are on my bookshelves. Rather, my goal is brevity, to tell the story in two hundred pages. This will give a taste and flavor of the subject and may hopefully help to understand a neighbor's religion, develop tolerance and foster pluralism.

May God give me the strength, courage and wisdom to produce an intelligent manuscript, in a brief understanding way.

1

BCE

✦

Before the Common Era

In writing a book on the history of religion I do so with the premise that man is basically a religious being. There was so much he had no control over. If he didn't know of a God, he created one. The Greeks created many Gods, there were an untold number of Pagan Gods and Gods even in the deepest jungles of far reaching lands, Gods were necessary to maintain life by controlling the weather, birth and provide food. They felt that Gods often required sacrifices such as animals or young maidens. My wife and I viewed the ancient ruins in Mexico and were shown the altars where human sacrifices were made. It is hard to visualize how one human being could burn another human being on an open fire so that a particular God would make the weather behave. But this is another subject which I leave to anthropologists and theologians. It has been very difficult to separate religious beliefs from historical accuracy and approach this book with an open mind.

I start this layman's history of religion with a synopsis of the basic groups that make up the formation years or sometimes referred to as the axial years of the first religions for which we will follow the schisms as they occur. A good place to start is with the Jewish Testament or biblical recordings of the history of their God. It was in about 2000 BCE that Abraham proclaimed that there is but one God who they referred to as Yahweh. The God described by Abraham was not recorded until 700 BCE. The Christians, two thousand years after

Abraham, proclaimed the God described by Abraham as the Father of the Trinity with Jesus and the Holy Ghost. Still, seven hundred years later after the death of Christ, Mohammed based his revelations on the God of Abraham, who he called Allah, the one and only one God. Even though the story and revelation of Abraham was not recorded until about 800 or 700 BCE, the author is unknown. It would be twelve hundred years after the fact that someone recorded the story. It is no wonder that historians question the very existence of Abraham.

On what was the other side of the world, in the days when the history of Abraham was recorded, there flourished in India another concept, still powerful and influential today, which was the basis of the Hindu religion. It had originated around 3000 BCE with ninety percent of its followers still living in India. Its founder is lost in the distant past and as a result it has no originator as all the other religions do. Priests and teachers of Brahman, the universal God, teach their concept of God, which reveals a right way of living (Dharma). This is a triad, however, with Brahma, Vishnu and Shiva, of which Brahma is the Chief. It is unique in that there are many theologies and sects. Historically, around 1500 BCE in the Indus Valley, the center of Hinduism was invaded by the Indo-Europeans, called Aryans, who spoke Sanskrit and transformed the Hindu Religion. In 1200 BCE the Rg-Veda was composed (a collection of over one thousand hymns). It was dedicated to many Gods of which Indra God of war and rain was the most popular. Angi was the God of fire and so on through many Gods. Most of the details are lost in time. This is the oldest Religious Scripture in the world. Between 800 and 600 BCE it was enlarged with prose, called the Upanishads.

The caste system is unique to India. It originally separated the people into priests (Brahmins), warriors, merchants and servants. It was expanded many times, down to the level of untouchables. The groups are hereditary. Common in the various divisions of Hinduism is reincarnation, called Samara, the process of birth and rebirth, life after life. There are conditions, however, whereby this process can be stopped.

An interesting aspect is that if you have lived wickedly, or not maintained the good, you may come back as a lesser creature.

In about 400 BCE a new denomination or schism was introduced called Jainism. This group was dedicated to not harming a living thing, but is basically Hinduism, and they are still active today. This concept came from the Jainism objection to living sacrifices and was carried out to the extreme.

Also in India, a wealthy man called Gautama grew up in the princely splendor of the upper class as a Hindu. In his travels he became aware of the poor and he started to search for the truth, most commonly referred to as the Good. He is said to have meditated for forty-nine days and received enlightenment to the riddle of life. As he broke away from Hinduism, which was a Protestant revolt against Orthodox Hinduism, he was then called the Buddha (the enlightened one). He is not God, but rather Gautama is a person to whom they show homage, always striving toward Nirvana, the ultimate reality. Meditation has always been an integral part of Buddhism. At one point Buddha so starved himself, that he fainted and was found unconscious on a road. A shepherd woman poured goat milk into his mouth and saved him. From that time on he taught that it is wrong to starve the body to extreme.

The earlier Buddhism was strictly an ethical religion. Two Sects developed, however, in which Mahayana changed to a Theist format wherein rituals, temples, shrines and monasteries developed. The other Sect Hinayana remained devoted to an ethical religion, very near to the original teachings of the Buddha. As contrasted to religious beliefs that the earth was created and will have an ending, Buddhism professes that the universe is not from beginning to end, but circular, with no beginning or ending. It has always been there and always will. It exists from a beginningless past to an endless future. This concept is part of Yoga thoughts or often called tradition that meditates on the good and the mysteries of life.

The original teachings of Buddha were recorded in what is called the Pali Cannon or the Tipitaka which contained the scriptures. They were divided into three parts, the Vinya, the Sutta and the Abhidhamma, all of which gave instructions or directions for the rules of the Monks and other doctrines for seeking Nirvana. Not all Monks reached Nirvana even after all requirements were accomplished. These are called Bodhisattva, one who has attained enlightenment but not Nirvana in order to help others. These individuals are greatly honored.

Edward Conzi explains in his book <u>Buddhism</u> that the ultimate reality is as follows, and I quote: "Nirvana is permanent, stable, imperishable, immovable, ageless, deathless, and unbecome, that is power, bliss and happiness, the secure refuge, the shelter and the place of unassailable security, that is the real truth and the supreme reality that is the good, the supreme goal and the one and only consummation of our life, the eternal, hidden and incomprehensible peace."

I leave the explanation of the above to theologians and philosophers and will later comment on the comparison between statements made by Jesus and the Buddha. There are some striking similarities. In his book <u>Jesus and Buddha</u>, Marcus Borg states that if the Buddha and Jesus were to meet, neither would try to convert the other.

Buddhism later immigrated to China and was joined by Confucianism and Taoism. They are the three pillars of religious philosophy in China and they are defined as Confucian Philosophy—Taoist Mysticism and Buddha's Metaphysics (a deductive way of understanding). To demonstrate how interrelated these are, an official was said to have died and was buried with the writings of Confucius and Taoism in his left hand and the Buddha text in his right hand. According to the book <u>The World's Great Religions</u> he died typical Chinese.

Confucius' teachings did not define a religion or describe the supernatural. He did, however, as a teacher, influence the people of China. He established rules to live by and shape the lofty system of ethics by which China lived and he developed a moral code of conduct.

Lao Tzo created Taoism which was an actual religion. In 604 BCE, Lao left his court post to travel and meditate. He is said to have, in a few days, composed the Bible of Taoism and then vanished over the mountain never to be seen again. Historians don't believe that it was written by one man but can't prove otherwise.

Another founder of an original religion was Zoroaster, in Persia. He was a priest in Persia, in the local religion, and he had worshipped the Gods of Sun, Moon, Earth, etc. He had a vision, however, from a God he called Ahura Mazoa who revealed one God. Thus was born Zoroastrianism, which claimed a revolutionary monotheism. The time period is after 1000 BCE or after Moses and before Gautama (the Buddha). According to Zoroaster, all are created to decide between good and evil, with evil leading to Hell. He also revealed a resurrection at judgment. It is this early definitive vision of Hell that makes this rather small group significant.

Moving once more in the same period, but this time in Greece, we find Pythagoras in the sixth century BCE. He was a Greek philosopher and mathematician and founder of the Pythagorean Brotherhood, which was religious in nature. He assembled ideas from India and Persia, however, and taught that reality is mathematical in nature. His work involved the first theory of functional significance of numbers in the world, and music. His followers, many years later, developed the Pythagorean Theory in geometry. He influenced Socrates in 469–399 BCE and Socrate's pupil Plato in 428–348 BCE, and finally Aristotle in 384–322 BCE, the student of Plato, who wrote long series of texts and important books on scientific rationalism. It is important for my purpose to historically place these philosophers in my chronology. The best-known Christian Platoist was St. Augustine of Hippo in 400 CE and later St. Thomas Aquinas in 1125–1175, or fourteen hundred years later and will combine Aristotle's scientific rationalism with Christian doctrine. Aristotle will also influence Islamic philosophy. He was the first to explain logical reasoning, the basis for all scientific reasoning. This metaphysical rationalism relies on reason as the best guide for belief and action. It is very important in that there is a strong effect on some major religious groups based on Abraham's one God. More influential in the early church in the area of Plato/Aristotle logic was the stoic logic. It is said to be more helpful to the Christians. In basic terms, the stoic logic (of the Megarian School) differed from Aristotle's in that the stoics introduced a more pragmatic approach. The stoic differences with Plato/Aristotle were actually one of emphasis. An interesting subject if one was not writing a history book.

This has been a thumbnail sketch of the creation or forming of the basic philosophies or religious tenants before the birth of Christ. Most authors use the term BCE (before Common Era) instead of BC (before Christ) and CE (Common Era) instead of AD (after death). This probably is due to the fact that Christianity elevates Christ to a position as God, while all others acknowledge Christ as an important prophet.

We are going to follow historically the many schisms (divisions) of these basic religions that will result from human nature, territorial conflict, treachery, misinterpretation, and the absence of love for thy neighbor. It would seem that the basic philosophies established for the major religions should cover the religious needs for all human souls. Nothing is further from the truth. They have fought wars and insurrections, suffered terrorism defending a religious point of view or the possession of a territory.

I do not wish to engage in theology but I can lay out a chronological order of how this all got started. I won't answer why, just when. I won't explain what is the good, just who attempted to do this. I profess no background in the study of theology and I represent myself as a layman in the Christian doctrine for which I have accumulated experience in the eighty years since my baptism. It is in the realm of intellectual curiosity that I make an effort to understand the cause for the strife between religions, which often leads to bloodshed in so many areas and in so many times.

Protestants and Catholics have fought for hundreds of years in Ireland. The Balkans are still a powderkeg with Catholic Croatians,

Orthodox Serbs and Albanian Muslims. The seven Holy Crusades over two hundred years were nothing more than the slaughter of human beings. Historians report that the later Crusades marched over the bones of the last Crusades. I feel a layman can ask, what were the circumstances when Augustine declared that war can be holy? Why did God instruct his early prophets to slaughter whole nations with not a survivor, just to gain territory and then put the captive kings to death.

At times I feel most inadequate for the task. It is humbling to realize how little we know of other religions, but I have a firm conviction that there is a need to chronologically look at the world's religious developments from the eye of a layman, making it mandatory to try to learn in the simplest, easiest and most understandable format.

Abraham, an Israelite, is credited with the basic tenet of the religions of the Jews, Muslims and Christians. He proclaimed that there is one God, and only one God. Of the three, only the Christians divide God into three separate identities, but together they are one God. Christianity, however, does not come on the scene for over two thousand years after Abraham, and Islam for 2700 years. We are discussing long periods of time.

Historically, how do we know of Abraham and his revolutionary ideas? There is no historical record; it comes only from the old Testament of the Jewish Bible, which is a collection or assembly of ancient scribe's stories about their ancestral background. The first books of the Bible seem to have a goal of defining nature, the law, and it is historical. In the case of the Hindus they define a way of living. The Buddha, or the enlightened one, a search for the good. Plato, Socrates and Aristotle have attempted the same phenomena through logic and reason.

The authors of the first books of the Bible are unknown. There is, however, an established identification of these authors. The earliest books, Genesis, Exodus, Leviticus, Numbers, and Deuteronomy were known as the Pentateuch and also as the Torah (the law section of the old Testament) These books were written about 800 to 600 BCE, over a thousand years after Abraham. The Judean author was designated "J" from the fact that he described God as Yahweh. "E" a northern Israeli source describes God as Elohim. The Deuteronomist as "D." and the priestly writings as "P," about the early history. There is a lack of similarity or structure in the writings, which is obvious to historians. The sentences or structure don't follow the same explanation or style, which makes it obvious that there were different authors. It does appear, however, that one individual or group assembled all the written documents, a hundred years or so after they were written, and made them into a smooth text or history by arranging the various author's writings into a chronological order to tell the story of Jewish history. This was a tremendous time gap of hundreds of years, if not a millennium, before these events were recorded, and we don't even know who wrote them. There are those fundamentalists who credit Moses with the authorship of all five books, but the modern historians do not. Abraham is often referred to as starting Israeli tradition, with Moses as the greatest hero who gave the world the Ten Commandments. Moses is portrayed as the true founder of Judaism because he instituted all the rituals and the Ark of the Covenant that contains the tables of the law and a priesthood to enforce it. You will note that I will bypass the mystical period that includes creation, the flood, etc.

I am, however, compelled to drop back into the mystical period for a comment on the flood and Noah's Ark, based on logical reasoning of a mystical event. I do this from a pragmatic view. I do so meaning no disrespect to the fundamentalists like my dear friends of many years ago, who I will call the Methodist and the Baptist. One example of their difference of opinion in interpreting the Bible is, one said that the Bible proves conclusively that he is not permitted to work on Sunday, and he didn't. The other proved conclusively that when your job required it you had to work on Sunday, which he did. Many very good discussions and endless assessments were made, but they never, over a period of six years, came to an agreement about anything. They both believed every word in the printed testament, both old and new, but interpreted it differently. I always explain that it didn't bother me or distract from my faith, that one of the stories, like Noah's Ark, was recorded after the fact. Someone writing three thousand years later obviously embellished it, who had no scientific knowledge or any facts to start with, and whose total scope of geography was limited to Mesopotamia and the Euphrates Valley.

It should be noted that in one place in the bible Noah is instructed to take a pair of each of the animals, but in another place he is to take seven of the unclean animals and two of the clean animals, indicating two authors combined into one story. Let me lay out some facts that would indicate to me, if not to my two friends, that the biggest or most significant miracle was not the Ark or the fact that Noah lived, but the control of the biological aspects of the animals. Consider the distance the animals had to come, unless we are just discussing the domestic animals. Convincing a pair of lions in Africa, polar bears in Alaska, or Bengal tigers in India, to walk quietly, orderly, obediently and quickly, to the middle East before it started to rain, is a bit of a stretch of the imagination. The storyteller was not aware of the existence of these rather domineering creatures of the wild. His descriptions quickly narrow in scope if he means all of Noah's domestic animals. These would be the horses, cows, camels, oxen, dogs, cats, poultry, birds, etc. There would be no pigs because the Jews did not eat pork. If the residents of the Ark extended to even the center of African animals, where would all the food be stored, and more important, drinking water. A cow would normally drink twelve gallons of water a day, and a camel doesn't drink often but needs to drink much when he does. A cow eats at least a quarter bale of hay a day and one half ton of water per month. The worst problem of all, which I can recognize, being somewhat of a cattleman, is that the larger animals, like cows, produce ten tons of manure a year and expel flatulence or gas at an alarming rate. Since the Ark was sealed this would have been a ghastly experience. The story teller did not consider this because he was not aware of it, as we would be today, with modern science determining that Pfiesteria Piscicida Toxic Microbe, or Cryptosporidium Organisms, are both due to animal waste, which in this length of time in a sealed building, would become critical, resulting in death. As a matter of comparison the story teller could not have visualized that the boat he is describing (300 cubits x 50 cubits wide) is only half as long as a Caribbean cruise ship today, and one third as wide and much smaller than a fifteen hundred foot oil tanker.

The next problem would take place when the family and animals exit from the Ark. They would have nothing to eat. The only mention of food from the storyteller is that after Noah waited for the ground to dry up he planted a vineyard. It is assumed, therefore, that Noah had the wisdom or God's instructions, to take grapevine cuttings with him on the Ark. It would have taken a full season of growth to grow food. Grapevines would take two years to produce grapes. It does make good wine, and Noah is later found drunk.

Now consider the poor animals when they are released from the Ark, in the mud, they would have nothing to eat because everything was destroyed. The lion would have to eat the zebra, which would be the end of them, the fox would eat the chicken, etc. Consider the disruption of the whole ecological system. The biggest miracle of all therefore, is that God kept the animals from eating or drinking water until the tenth month, when the tops of the mountains were seen. Noah waited 40 more days to send a raven out and also a dove but it was another week before the dove brought back a branch to indicate the waters were drying up. This totals almost a year in which no gas was expelled and they were too weak to fight. In addition, God would have to provide food for Noah and his family and feed all the animals for another year.

The whole story sounds more logical if Noah had only his farm animals to contend with while the wild animals sought shelter by climbing to higher places. This is not to say that the story did not happen according to God's will, it is just the fact that the story teller is writing about an incident that happened a couple of thousand years before he was born, and we don't even know who the author was.

There is a book called <u>Noah's Flood</u> written by Ryan and Pitman (Columbia University Geologist) which describes a really large flood in the area of the Black Sea approximately 7500 years ago. Recently, scientists have discovered that five hundred feet below the water line of the Black Sea lies an old shoreline. It confirms the basis of a flood of Biblical proportions, which was described several thousand years after the fact, but indicates that it was confined to this area. This again suggests that many of the Bible's stories should not be taken in great detail, but consider that they were written long after the fact and by someone of unknown source.

One very interesting fact is recorded by the German philosopher Karl Jaspers in the <u>Origin and Goal of History</u> in which he refers to the Axial Period, 800 to 300 BCE, in which all the main religions of the civilized world were recorded and created new ideologies that have continued to be critical and influential. These are the Hindus, Greek Philosophers, Buddha, Confucius, Taoism, Zoroastrians and the Hebrew Prophets. All of the chief civilizations developed along parallel lines although there was no commercial contact between China and the European area. No one really understands why or how this happened.

We can follow the biblical events starting with Abraham for which much has been corroborated by Archaeologists. Abraham's Clan, in around 1800 BC moved about in order to always have water and pasture for their flocks. His sons Isaac and Jacob were said to be rich with large flocks while Joseph, who had been sold into slavery, became in a short thirteen years, Grand Vizier of Egypt (Keeper of the Grain Supplies).

In 1700 BCE a new King of Egypt grew to hate the Israelites and called them Nomads or Sand Dwellers. It was convenient for him to turn them into slaves to make bricks and used as general labor to build the Pharaoh's gigantic structures.

In 1280 to 1220, Moses would lead the Israelites out of Egypt. How many is not known but historians say there may have been several groups. The translation of the words Red Sea in Exodus, according to historians, should have been Sea Of Reeds which if true, it was not the Red Sea that Moses crossed but rather the Sea of Reeds. Scholars still cannot agree on the location. They speculate that the very large group of Jews used the northern route through a marshy area as the suggested location of the Sea of Reeds. It would be possible to cross by foot or handcarts but the heavy Egyptian chariots would not be able to cross. The bible clearly states that God parted the water and held it back until the Egyptians arrived with their war chariots. This then becomes a matter of faith.

Moses, after forty years, never reached his destination, but rather left that to his son Joshua, who scouted the sought after land and planned his assault on the inhabitants, one small country at a time. One of his assaults was at Jericho, where scholars point out there had not been any walls for three hundred years, because invaders had destroyed them. It seems from today's view, that it wouldn't have been necessary to massacre all the inhabitants but that it was God's orders. This was true according to biblical reports at Jericho, Ai and Hazor. Archaeologists, through their work show that only the Hazor incident is accurate because it was burned during this time period.

The wars with Israelite neighbors continued and finally Gideon took charge and made war against the Midiate rulers and slew them all.

One of the judges was Samuel, but he and his sons proved unable to rule so the task fell to Saul, a warrior taller and more handsome than any of his people. It was the Philistines to the northeast that made it important for the twelve tribes to select a king. Saul proved to be a good general but he failed to complete the Lord's orders to kill everything and everybody at Amalekete, so he was rebuked and rejected as a King.

In Bethlehem, Samuel, seeking a new king, found David, son of Jesse, and eventually anointed him King (the story leading up to this was David fighting Goliath, a ten foot tall giant). In 961 BCE David was made ruler of Israel, which he would govern for thirty-three years.

He made Jerusalem his capital after capturing it from the Jebusites, and it became the City of David. David brought the Ark of the Covenant to Jerusalem. Solomon, David's second son, replaced him.

It should be noted here that archaeologists have found ancient slates inscribed with "King of Israel" and "House of David." From this find, at least some of the archaeologists concede that there really was a David and the recorded biblical story is at least partially true.

Solomon is said to have been the most splendid Prince to rule Israel. While David brought the Ark, Solomon built the structure to house it. He reigned from 961 to 922 BCE.

After Solomon, the Kingdom was divided in two, and soon after, the Egyptians fought their way north in 918. Many rulers and battles followed but in 745 BCE the Assyrian forces captured Israel with a desire to expand their kingdom and assimilate the captive people into their society.

The Israeli people felt trapped between the Assyrian forces and the Egyptian forces, which resulted in a deal with Tiglath-Piles III, King of Assyria, to be cooperative in order to gain protection from surrounding enemies.

After a long period of submission, the Jews were slowly slipping from tradition and religious dedication. Under the leadership of Josiah they had a religious reformation reverting back to circumcision and forbidding mixed marriages. He also extended their territory but the Assyrians were getting weaker and the Egyptians were moving north. The Jewish army tried to stop them but the Egyptians destroyed the Army of Judah. During the battle, Josiah was wounded and died in Jerusalem. It is said, "Judah died with him."

By 589 BCE the new enemy was the Babylonian Army who overran Judah and surrounded Jerusalem. The excavated caves reveal the horrors of the long assault. In the summer of 587 all hope was lost, the city fell and the Babylonians gathered up thousands to be deported to Babylon as slaves. This was four hundred years after King David and five hundred years before Jesus. Judah came to an inglorious end.

Archeologists have found that evidence of the massive destruction of Jerusalem, once splendid, was uninhabitable. Many Jews, which name they first received at this time, escaped to surrounding countries. Even Egypt, a former enemy, became a home to many. The Jews in time became part of Egypt's commercial trade.

The Babylonians allowed Jews to settle in villages, which assured the survival of the Jewish people. Other Jews were spread throughout Assyria and were often called the ten lost tribes.

By 539 BCE the Kingdoms of Egypt and Babylonia were in disarray. The Persian Army took advantage of this and destroyed the Babylonian Army. The Jewish people felt that this was the answer to their prayer to the Lord, because Cyrus the Persian leader allowed the Jews to remain in their villages. He did not follow the Assyrian and Babylonian system of conquering people by moving them, but showed tolerance and allowed the Jews to return to Judah. He also ordered the Temple in Jerusalem to be rebuilt and provided the financial means to get it started. When the small band of Jews finally reached Jerusalem they found the ruins much more extensive than they had envisioned. It was not until more Jewish groups and much political intrigue in the Persian government that the Temple was completed. It did not resemble the original temple that Solomon built, and had no fortification.

The next significant period was around 440 BCE with the rule of Nehemiah, a Persian official as Governor, and Esra as spiritual leader. The rule against intermarriage was again established and enforced. The Sabbath observance was honored. Esra read the law to the people of Jerusalem, which was at least part of what is known as the Torah. A law was passed by the Rabbi that all mixed marriages were dissolved. Some obeyed, some moved on or ignored the order.

By this time in history there was extensive trade and commerce, resulting in the establishment of many Greek Ports with influence on all the trade routes. There is very little historical documentation during these years until the arrival of Alexander the Great.

Alexander the Great was born in 356 BCE to King Philip II of Macedonia. As a young man, Alexander started as an officer in his father's army. It is reported that Alexander commanded all the troops on his father's left wing during battles, which taught him warfare in battle conditions. He set out to conquer the known world, and did, in eleven years. He captured and defeated army after army until he established control all around the Mediterranean world. He reached Egypt in 332 BCE where he freed Egypt from Persian rule and became Pharaoh. He built the City of Alexandria, which is important because it became the largest Jewish City, thriving with commerce. It did, however, start some different views within the Jewish religion. This period is referred to by historians as the Hellenistic Age, which means, "act like a Greek." During this period Greek culture and language spread throughout the whole Mediterranean world. During Alexander's massive exploiting of the known world, there were with him, on all his expeditions, botanists, scientists, and mapmakers, to plot his acquired territory. They were emissaries of Aristotle and provided a constant flow of data back to him. He was able to send these emissaries because Alexander was a student of Aristotle in the Macedonian Court. It was Alexander who provided the funds for Aristotle to set up his school in Athens, called the Peripatetic School. It is interesting to note that the name means "walk around" based on the fact that Aristotle would walk around the school gardens discussing science with his advanced students. After Egypt, Alexander was made King of Asia and was welcomed in Persia and Babylon. He reached India but returned to Babylon where he died of fever in June of 323 BCE at the age of thirty-three.

The Septuagint, in approximately 200 BCE, was a translation into Greek from the Hebrew Bible. It was started after 300 BCE and finished after 200 BCE. It was most significant in that it was prepared for the Jews that were scattered in the world, (the scattering was called Diaspora). According to legend, six representatives from each of the twelve Hebrew tribes, or a total of seventy-two authors, contributed to the writing of the Septuagint. This translation was used by later scholars as one of the important documents to assemble and translate the Bible as we know it today.

In reference to the twelve tribes of Israelites, most Jews claim descendancy from only Judah and Benjamin. The other tribes, Asher, Naftali, Reuven, Gad, Ephraim, Dan, Zevulun, Issachar, Simeon, and Levi have long been considered lost tribes. The Assyrians (now Syria) had conquered the kingdom of Israel around 600 BCE. Many Jews were made slaves while many fled to other distant lands, and settled in small numbers so as to blend in. In modern times came Simcha Jacobovici, a Canadian documentary filmmaker who traveled in the middle East and Asia to find pockets of Jewish inhabitants that he identified as nine of the ten missing tribes. This is 2700 years after the fact and Jewish Rabbis were not impressed and contended that Simcha produced no evidence to associate these isolated Jews to particular ancient tribes.

After Alexander's death his Generals divided the conquered world into Ptolemies in Egypt, the Seleucids in Asia, Asia Minor and Palestine and the Antigonids in Macedonia and Greece. All named after the Generals. The Ptolemies lasted the longest until the Romans arrived in 30 BCE.

Philo of Alexandria, the Jewish philosopher of that day, was influenced in his writing by the Hellenistic Age, and Judaism in turn was deeply influenced by the Greek Philosophers and Alexander.

It was during this very tumultuous time, starting about 200 BCE, that the Essens, a Jewish Sect, became organized into a viable entity. This bit of history was downplayed until the famous Dead Sea Scrolls which belong to this group were found in 1947. This is an important Schism because it is a break with Jewish tradition. The Essens were no doubt influenced by Hellenistic influence. To what extent, I leave to the theologians. Little is known about them because of their secret lifestyle.

While under Syrian rule the Jewish leadership started to object to the Greek influence into their lives, and started a major uprising during which time they attempted to recapture Jerusalem. This struggle is recorded in the four books of the Maccabees. Basically it is a story of Judas Maccabee, their leader, who fought and received independence from Syria and recaptured Jerusalem, starting in 164 BCE. It was then again the center of an independent state, which brought many Jews back that had been exiled by the conquerors of Palestine, or attracted by foreign trade. These were the Jews called Diaspora (exiled or scattered).

Starting in 55 BCE the Jews were ruled by a king from the Herod Dynasty. This all started when the Maccabian John Hyrcanus forced the area Governor Antipater to become Jewish by becoming circumcised and accepting Judaism. None of the Herods were actually Jewish by birth. Antipater became ruler of all of Palestine in 43 BCE, by a grant from Caesar. One of his children was Herod the Great or the First. This is the Herod at the time of Jesus' birth, who started to rebuild the Temple in Jerusalem around 20 BCE and also a new seaport. He was a mean individual, however. After Augustus made him King of the Jews, he proved his gruesome character by murdering his wife, her grandfather, and some of his own children. This character lends credence to the story of Herod ordering the death of infants to eliminate any possible rival because Jesus as an infant had been called King of the Jews. This incident is not found anywhere except in the account in the Gospel.

One of the seven Herods, Herod Antipas, was the son of Herod the Great. He was Tetrarch of Galilee who is most mentioned in the Bible. This is the Herod who sent Jesus to Pontius Pilate, who pronounced him guilty of treason.

By 64 BCE Rome had annexed Palestine, Syria and Mesopotamia and finally Egypt by 30 BCE. This now sets the stage for the Christian schism.

The Jews were a constant threat to the Romans, which resulted in many cruelties to the Jewish people who often fought back.

John the Baptist no doubt was influenced by the Essens, as several of Jesus' disciples may have been. Consider that here is a preacher out in the desert attracting multitudes. What was his message? It is a break with the Jewish Temple, which is a major schism. People would not come out in those numbers to be baptized, unless he presented a fresh new approach to religion. If all he says is that someone is to follow me, they would no doubt say, call us when he gets here. He had to have presented what would soon become the Christian religion. The sermons and preaching that he presented I leave to the theologians, but in my opinion, they handled John's message with reluctance. They feared that it would lessen Jesus' message, which it would not.

Before moving into the beginning of Christianity, It should be noted that the Jewish religion or tradition, was somewhat segmented by rival groups, which perhaps offered fertile territory for Christianity. The groups are as follows: Pharisees, who were strict adherents to the law, but also the oral interpretation of tradition. The Sadduces were the priests of the temple who attempted to preserve Jewish tradition by cooperating with the Roman authority. They were different from the Pharisees in that they did not accept oral traditions or interpretations of the law. It is believed that the Essens did influence John the Baptist and at least some of Jesus' disciples. It is interesting to note that Jesus condemned both the Pharisees and Sadduces, but there is not one mention of the Essenes in the Bible. This diversity of thought and doctrine no doubt contributed to the spark of Christianity with John the Baptist preaching in the desert against Jewish tradition and the coming of Jesus the Christ.

Chronology of Chapter I

1500	Abraham is the first Hebrew patriarch recognizing one and only one God.
1500	The Vedic of Hymns which contains the Hindu Rg-Veda is the oldest known Religious text.
1225	Hebrew exodus from Egypt led by Moses.
1000	Zoroaster founds Zoroastrianism in the Middle East.
940	First Temple in Jerusalem built by Solomon.
850	First books of the Old Testament are recorded.
600	First proverbs were written.
586	Destruction of Jerusalem and capture of Judah by Babylonia, Jews taken into slavery.
580	Pythagoras of Samos, develops mathematical harmonies.
550	Books of Genesis through Kings are edited to form the First History of the Hebrews.
551	Confucius teaches virtue and moral conduct.
521	Siddhartha Gautama 583–483 became Buddha in a search for the truth.
483	First Buddhist conference is held in India to write texts.
474	(399) Socrates in Athens studies the nature of virtue.
428	(348) Plato founded a school of philosophy introducing political theory.
400	(300) Jainism was introduced in India.
384	(322) Aristotle from Macedonia spent twenty years in Plato's school. Founded a school of his own in Athens. He was the teacher of Alexander the Great.
356	Alexander the Great is born.
340	Buddhist movement is split into Mahayana (Greater) vehicle and Hinayana (Lesser).
330	Alexander reaches Egypt.
323	Alexander died in Babylon.
200	Jewish Septuagint translated Hebrew Old Testament into Greek.

Chronology of Chapter I
(Continued)

200	Start of Essens movement.
200	Buddhism spreads to central Asia.
200	Informal Canons of Confucian classics is developed.
165	Judas Maccabees defeats Syrians and rededicates the Temple in Jerusalem.
150	Ecclesiastics is written, which completes the Old Testament.
141	Confucius is elevated to Saint and Confucianism is taught in public schools.
135	Pharisees are opposed by Sadducees which results in strife and Roman intervention.
64	Rome annexed Palestine, Syria and Mesopotamia.
55	The start of the Herod dynasty.
30	Rome captures Egypt.
20	John the Baptist starts his ministry to lead the way for Jesus.
20	Herod the Great starts rebuilding the temple in Jerusalem.
7	Birth of Jesus.

2

0–300 CE

❖

The Early Christians

The life of Jesus starts the second of the three most significant individuals who created and gave life to the entire Christian movement. We spoke of John the Baptist who led the way by preaching to multitudes and baptizing them. Jesus said of John, "there is no greater man born to woman." The details of John's preaching are not known but this is a major schism in Jewish tradition.

Jesus preached and taught the new religious edicts or sacramental tenets of the Christian faith. He did not, however, lay out a church structure, but rather left this to Paul, the most influential of the apostles, the third significant individual. Jesus taught and preached for three years. He was only 30 years old, but this was not a young man in those days. Some historians say that he may have preached only one year. Some suggest that he may have toured India and its surrounding areas prior to his ministry, but this is pretty much disproved. The reason for this mysterious trip through India is that a number of Jesus' teachings and the recorded scripture of Buddha are strikingly similar. In his book Jesus and Buddha, Marcus Borg points out that many ideas are identical even if they are five hundred years apart, three thousand miles apart, and included two drastically different cultures. These facts no doubt started some historians wondering if Jesus did visit in India. After all, his whereabouts are unaccounted for from age twelve to thirty.

Some examples taken from the book <u>Jesus and Buddha</u> show a similarity in loving your enemies, turning the other cheek, one who lives by the sword will die by the sword, all of which are mirrored in the words of Buddha. Some examples:

> Jesus: Do to others, as you would have them do to you.
> Buddha: Consider others as yourself.
> Jesus: If anyone strikes you on the cheek offer the other also.
> Buddha: If anyone should give you a blow with his hand, or with a knife, you should abandon any desires and utter no evil words.
> Jesus: Put your sword back in its place: For all those who take the sword will perish by the sword.
> Buddha: Abandoning the taking of life, the ascetic Gautama dwells on refraining from taking life with stick or sword.
> Jesus: This is my commandment, that you love one another as I have loved you. No one has greater love than this, to lay down ones life for ones friends.
> Buddha: Just as a Mother would protect her only child at the risk of her own life, even so cultivate a boundless heart towards all beings. Let your thoughts of boundless love pervade the whole world.

There are 114 similar quotations, which does make one wonder or at least historically curious.

Jesus selected twelve men to follow him and in reality to create his Church. Jesus never wrote a line to record anything. Much of his teaching was in parables, which Jesus explained to his disciples were a means of reaching those that believe, and those that don't will not understand the meaning or profit from his teaching. Jesus spoke the Aramaic language, which was the language of his native Galilee. Scholars believe he probably knew Hebrew and some Greek.

As the Christmas story relates, Jesus was born in Bethlehem, but some historians believe that he was born in Nazareth. The only thing that the four gospels agree on is that Jesus was a Nazarene and grew up in that small village and became a carpenter. Only Matthew mentions the Star of David and the Wise Men. Only Luke mentions the angels and shepherds. Some historians question the whole Christmas story that Joseph would go to Bethlehem to be taxed. As only reported in Luke, they point out that the Romans would not stop work to collect taxes. In addition, they point out that it would be improbable that Joseph would take Mary on such a long trip of sixty-two miles on foot or on a donkey in her last weeks of pregnancy. The Christmas story is such a beautiful children's story, that historians are reluctant to publish these facts. The important thing is that there is a Jesus regardless of where he was born.

The story in Luke as contrasted to Matthew's story of escaping from Herod by going to Egypt, only Luke reports that there was no room in the inn and that there was a manger in which Jesus was born. After which they took Jesus to the Temple to be blessed and circumcised and then returned home to Nazareth.

Only in Matthew do we find that God's instruction to Joseph was to take the baby Jesus to Egypt to escape the wrath of King Herod. He was in the process of killing male babies to make sure he destroyed the child who was referred to as King of the Jews. The skeptics look at the trip as unreliable information because why would Joseph travel 240 miles up the Nile and back in three and a half years or a total of 480 miles. It would be logical that Joseph would select a town where he could work and support his family. Saint Theophilus of the Coptic Church (Christian), wrote this account five hundred years into the common era, or after the death of Jesus. The church leaders admit that it is based on faith. They pray that archaeologists can find some small evidence to clarify or confirm this story, but none have been found. The designated holy locations along the 480 miles attract many pilgrims and many of the churches along the way depend on the tourist trade for their existence.

Mark and John start their gospel at the time of John the Baptist's meetings with Jesus at the Jordan River.

The Christmas story as told and celebrated in Christian Churches today is a compilation of facts from stories and chosen traditions that have survived through two thousand years.

Some historians contend that it is not surprising that the authors wrote contradicting stories forty to one hundred years after the death of Jesus but none had first hand information and each was attempting to fulfill prophecies from the Old Testament.

There is no record of Jesus' young years except in Luke wherein it is written that Jesus went at age twelve to the temple in Jerusalem to discuss Hebrew theology with the elders. After this we have no record except that he became a carpenter and set out to preach when he was around thirty years old.

Jesus' travels were confined to a relatively small area in today's reference. The area is approximately twenty-five miles wide and three hundred miles long, which when traveling by foot or by donkey is very difficult and even dangerous. The area covers two main tours in a total Holy Land area about the size of the state of New Jersey. When we discuss destinations for tours, distances are important to the main points of reference.

Alexandria is on the Mediterranean coast of Egypt and is about three hundred miles to Jerusalem. In the other direction, at the far end of the Mediterranean is Antioch, which is about three hundred miles from Jerusalem. These cities were important because they were each the base of a Patriarch in the early church. Bethlehem is a little over two miles from Jerusalem and Jesus' home in Nazareth is approximately sixty-two miles from Jerusalem. As the crow flies, Rome is approximately fourteen hundred miles from Jerusalem and that is not exactly next door, especially in the unreliable galleys that crossed the Mediterranean. It is a much longer trip around the end of the Mediterranean.

Why did the Jewish leaders reject Jesus? He was not the Messiah that they had expected or the King that they anticipated. Here was a carpenter's son, referred to as Mary's son, which would imply a bastard son because he would normally be called Joseph's son if all were normal. In addition the mighty King coming to save the Jews from the Romans, was riding into Jerusalem on a donkey. He had condemned the Jewish church itself. What kind of a Messiah was this? The way was cleared to get rid of this upstart, or thorn in their side, by just not objecting to the Romans crucifying him and waiting for the real Messiah, the one in their mind's eye. Modern Jews will say that we do not live in a messianic age because we still have wars and hatred in the world. They will wait for the Messiah, which will bring a messianic age free of war and hatred.

The disciples whom Jesus chose were not as some have claimed, illiterate fishermen, but rather selected from the common people. He could have selected Greek scholars or any number of men with advanced learning. Perhaps Jesus did not want disciples who were already indoctrinated into a man created knowledge of good and evil, or the Gnosticism that was soon to proliferate in that area. His choices were as follows:

> **Peter (Simon)**: A fisherman in Capernaum, a native of Bethsaida, he was partner with James and John.
> **Andrew**: Peter's brother, also a fisherman, a follower of John the Baptist.
> **James**: Son of Zebedee, also a fisherman.
> **John**: Son of Zebedee, younger brother of James.
> **Philip**: From Galilee, not Philip the Evangelist.
> **Bartholomew**: From Cana, a friend of Philip, preached in Parthia.
> **Thomas**: Also called Didymus, missionary to Parthia.
> **Matthew**: Also called Levi, from Capernaum.
> **James**: Son of Alphaeus, brother of Matthew.
> **Simon**: The Canaanite.
> **Judas**: Iscariot (who betrayed Jesus) was replaced by Mattais.
> **Thaddeus**: Companion of Jesus, might be called Lebbaeus.

The authorship of the books of the New Testament is either vague or unknown. It is probably true that none of the twelve disciples wrote the books of the New Testament. Paul and Luke were educated in Roman schools. Paul wrote more than half of the New Testament and Luke two of the most important books. If you add Mark who wrote the only actual history of Jesus life, an evangelist like Paul and Luke, you have the three most important individuals to author the Bible.

Matthew: This book was written in approximately CE 75–100. It was assigned to Matthew because the author was unknown. Ninety percent of this book is reproduced from Mark.

Mark: Written between 49 and 50. This is the shortest and simplest of the four Gospels. It records the life of Jesus and some say it is the only actual record. Matthew, Luke and John all depend on Mark, which formed the basis of the other three gospels.

Luke: Written around 75 (some say 58–60). Luke was a physician and friend of Paul. Luke was the only writer of the New Testament that was not a Jew.

John: Written around 100 by most likely an Elder known as John of Ephesus. John the Disciple was martyred in the year 70.

Acts: Completed around 75 along with the Gospel of Luke. The author was Luke.

Romans: Written around 56–58 by Paul.

Corinthians: Paul wrote Corinthians 1st and 2nd books around 56–58.

Galatians: Written in 50–57 by Paul. This was his earliest work.

Ephesians: Written 59–61 while Paul was in prison.

Philippians: Written 59–61 by Paul while he was in prison.

Thessalonians: 1st and 2nd books written in 50–53 by Paul.

Timothy: 1st and 2nd books written according to some scholars in 61–70, by Paul. Those who claim Paul died in prison in 61 establish this date. Others believe that he was released and traveled to Spain. He was then jailed and martyred in 68–70. Further questions arise because the three pastoral epistles, Timothy 1st and 2nd, plus Titus, were not completed until 100.

Titus: Written 68 CE by Paul. Like the books of Timothy, the date is either 61 or 70 depending on the dates he was in prison.
Philemon: Written 59–61 by Paul while he was in prison.
Hebrews: Author, place and date unknown.
James: Completed around 90, the author is unknown. It is the first of five Epistles called General (they are James, 1st and 2nd Peter, 1st John and Jude). Other sources contend James, brother of Jesus, authored it in 63.

Peter 1st and 2nd: Written in 81–96 but it is pseudonymous. Peter was martyred in 64 and this book discusses events in the persecution era in 81–96.

John 1st, 2nd and 3rd: Written, most likely, by John of Ephesus or any one of the Church elders. The date is unknown but scholars indicate it was written between 80–110. John was martyred in 70.
Revelations: Written after 100, most likely, by John of Ephesus.

Over a period of three years or however long Jesus was teaching and preaching, his disciples listened and made mental notes. It is acknowledged that Jesus chose not to write or document his sermons. It is also not justified to say that Jesus was illiterate. He was trained as a carpenter, a skilled craftsman, and without a doubt was instructed and acquired a knowledge of Hebrew scripture. Strangely, however, the twelve disciples never took notes or wrote a diary. In the New Testament book of Acts, Peter and John were referred to by the high priest as unlearned and ignorant. This does not mean that they were illiterate and could not write, but rather they were not of the priestly school of Rabbis, but were common men of ordinary education.

In all the history of the world no event results in such a great influence as those three years in a small remote area where Jesus preached, unknown to the rest of the world. His short ministerial service culminated with three days in Jerusalem where he was arrested and convicted of destroying property and treason. He was condemned by both the Roman and Jewish hierarchy and finally crucified. His followers met with him after he was raised from the dead. The result of this speck in history, now two thousand years later, is the basis of our calendar which dates from Jesus' birth, with two billion followers, and all from a handful of believers in a very revolt torn area.

In addition to the books of the new bible there are other important documents such as the Apostles Creed for which there does not seem to be any reliable historical fact regarding it's origin. It defined much of the church doctrine and was used from about 100 CE. It left some things unsaid and/or defined, which would be debated for six hundred years. The Lord's Prayer, the most used prayer in the Christian Church, originated as part of the Sermon on the Mount.

One other document written at this time is the Didache or teaching of the twelve Apostles. Written after 100 CE, to confirm praying to God through Jesus Christ and direct reference to Lord Jesus in prayer, plus moral teaching and church order.

A bit later, approximately 400 CE, the Athanasian Creed was developed. It contained 40 verses and deals with the trinity and incarnation. The author is still unknown and the creed itself is of minor use today. It is authoritative by the Roman Church and some Protestants. It is most explicit in its demand for strict adherence to its truth, or one would never attain salvation.

Still another important document in 500 CE for the Diaspora Jews (scattered) was the Vulgate. It was a translation to Greek, which could be read and understood by Jews throughout the world.

Historically, the third most significant individual to start and organize the Christian Church was Paul. His parents, although Jewish, had become Roman citizens. He was educated in Jerusalem and became a Jewish Rabbi. He had persecuted the Christian refugees, but was converted to Christianity by God, alone on a lonely road. He became aware of Jesus' teaching by listening to the followers of Jesus. He became an itinerant preacher, and according to Jacques Brose <u>Religious Leaders</u> he toured the pagan lands of Cypress, Asia Minor, Macedonia and Greece. Paul stands out because he stood firm in the fact that his friend Luke, a gentile, did not have to live by Jewish Law, part of which required circumcision. The Christians at that time were all Jews and were obedient to Jewish law. Paul led the way when Peter came to Antioch to discuss the issue of Gentiles joining the Church, but Peter was opposed. He returned to Jerusalem without concurring with Paul. Paul had "withstood him to the face" as recorded in Galatians. Paul and Barnabas went to Jerusalem to discuss the issue with Apostles and Elders. Paul won his point and Gentiles in Antioch and Alexander were excused from Jewish Law. This was the spark that ignited the Christian Church movement. The Jewish Christians as a group lasted for one hundred years and declined to an almost non-existence. Some still exist today as Messianic Jews who acknowledge the Messiah.

Nero (37–68) was the last Roman Emperor descended from Julius Caesar. He was a depraved tyrant. A common story tells about Nero fiddling while Rome burned in 64 CE. He instigated the first persecution of the Christians because, it is said, that he blamed the fire on the Christians. Other reports with a greater reliability say that he was not even in Rome at the time of the fire.

The Jews in Palestine at this time, approximately 60 CE, were faced with local government taxes, taxes to the Church and ever increasing taxes to Rome. In addition there were trade problems in that the Palestinians had to purchase, at a higher price, merchandise made in Rome. It is reported that the same year that Herod died, 1000 Israelites were crucified. The Jews organized an army that was dedicated to freeing Palestine from Roman tyranny.

Politics in Rome made it mandatory that the Palestinian revolt be stopped and come under strict Roman rule. It culminated with the Roman Titus arriving in Palestine with fifteen thousand well-armed men. This was in 66 CE and by 78 CE they had burned the Temple of Jerusalem. The only part left standing was the West Wall which Rabbis today still believe will be the cornerstone of the new Temple to be built by the Messiah when he returns.

The Jews fought a good fight for over ten years but were finally cornered on a steep hilltop called Masada. This was a fortification built to ward off any enemy and was well stocked with food, water and armaments. It took the Romans two years to reach the top by building a ramp roadway on which to move their destructive machines, such as rams and catapults, etc. The fortification fell in 73 CE and all but eleven of the one thousand Jews committed suicide rather than being captured to face ultimate crucifixion. This would be after killing the wives and children. Some Jews don't like the term suicide and refer to the incident as an expediency of the war. The fact remains that they did commit suicide, after ten years of fighting. The Romans killed approximately a total of 300,000 Jews and their Temple was destroyed.

The Romans were naturally annoyed after defeating the Jews because a new group called Christians was springing up everywhere in the area. To add insult to injury the Christians were infiltrating Rome itself. The High Priests of the Jews were likewise fearful of the new schism from their tradition.

Another reminder of this period is the Coliseum in Rome built in 82 CE under Flavien, to provide a place to entertain the Roman citizens. There was not much to do in those days except for the Roman baths, but how long can a Roman bathe. It was convenient that in addition to the Gladiator performances for entertainment they had Christians to murder in all forms of events. Lions were one of the favorite events. One or two whole families of Christians would be herded into the center of the arena, which would signal the release of three or four lions who had not eaten in several days. Those that died quickly were fortunate in not having to watch the lions eat their dear ones before it was their turn. On other occasions large numbers of starving lions were released. One of the favorite individual events according to an anonymous report, was chaining a Christian's legs to two separate horses and then whipping the horses to make them run in opposite directions, tearing the poor Christian in half. That was cruel entertainment.

Chronologically, the historical account of the origin of the Christian Church was as I have reported. John the Baptist led the way, with a great schism in the Jewish tradition. Jesus the Christ, whose teaching is the Christian faith, followed John. It took Paul, however, to have the vision of a universal church, open to all people, a church home for the gentiles, which in two millenniums has become the largest church on earth. From a practical standpoint it does appear that many people were looking for a new religion or at least were in a receptive mood.

Assembling the New Testament was not an easy or fast process, but essential to record the thoughts and words of the early Christians. Mark, who had traveled with Paul and Barnabas on their first missionary journey, wrote the first of the four canonical Gospels in 64 CE. It is after 100 CE before the Gospel of Matthew is written. St. John may not have been finished until after 125 and by 150 the four Gospels were completed. On or after 200, the New Testament was largely fixed.

Some historians refer to as many as twenty lost books of the bible. There is much written about them but they may not be lost at all. There is evidence that they are a duplicate, not accepted as authority (canon) or material incorporated into existing books. Two examples are the Book of Jashar and the Book of the Wars of Yahweth.

The period referred to as early Christianity was approximately 80 to 200 CE. This, the Amish in particular, referred to as the basis of their religion. The period 200 to 313 CE is filled with controversy between the leaders of the Christian Church. Many feel the early Christians still taught and wrote about the actual words of Jesus. In his book <u>Will the Real Heretics Please Stand Up</u> by David W. Burcot, he asserts that the early Christians would be indignant to be called Church Fathers. The most famous of these Church leaders or early Christians as they are referred to, are as follows:

> **Polycarp**: Disciple of the Apostle John, who appointed Polycarp overseer of the Church in Smyrna. He was martyred at the stake in 155 CE.

Irenaeus: Disciple of Polycarp, who served in France.

Clement of Alexandria: Philosopher turned Christian. His writings are a composite of his teachers and fellow writers.

Origin: At seventeen he was known for his brilliance. His lectures on the Bible became the first set of Bible commentaries. In charge of the training school, he replaced Clement at eighteen. Was tortured to death at age seventy.

Tertullian: Apologist to the Romans. He wrote in Latin rather than Greek, from 190 to 210. Later in life he joined and wrote about the Montanist Sect. The Amish only look at the first half of his writings. He is said to have had the greatest influence on the Christian Church from Paul to Augustine.

Ignasius: The Bishop of Antioch was martyred in Rome in 107 CE. Antioch is where the followers of Jesus were first called Christians.

Justin: Known as the Martyr, born a Pagan in Samaria, studied philosophy and Christianity. He wrote, "Faith does not contradict reason." Died in 165 CE.

The early Christians were writers, teachers, and leaders of the Church, through the roughest of times. Execution and martyrdom was common. With all the dreadful danger, the Church withstood it all. They met in private homes, changing locations so that no one could expose them. They also met in what was called the Catacombs in Rome. These were actually burying tombs for the Romans. In reality they were meeting in the Roman cemetery. It is interesting to note that meeting in private homes, women had a very involved participation in church activity. After Constantine and church buildings came into use, women's role in active influence was reduced. The Monks who followed asceticism (strict self-denial and spiritual discipline) and established the first celibacy contrived this. They also established Monasticism (Monasteries). Through the most difficult of times the early Christians managed to put into writing the very foundation of the new church.

All through this period a philosophical virus penetrated the basic concepts of the struggling early church. The most dangerous was Gnosticism, which the early Christians considered heretic. By the year 200 CE it had a rather large following which exercised a strong influence on both Judaism and Christianity. The name itself means "knowledge" and implies that salvation comes from insight or the capacity to discover truths by the help of your own intellect. Gnostics believe that Jesus was not truly a human being, he only appeared to be. He could not, as God, have died. Many of the ideas came from Plato and a variety of religious and philosophical trends in the Middle East. It is often referred to as dualism, good and evil, light and dark. It's purpose was to instruct it's followers as to Life's true nature. A whole library of Gnostic writings was found in a jar at Nag Hammed in 1945. They had been translated to Coptic (ancient Egyptian language) from Greek. The Dead Sea Scrolls belonging to the Essenes, dating back to 70 CE were discovered at Qumram in 1947.

There was an endless list of competing theology to the Early Church. The Essenes and the Gnostics which were mentioned, plus the Montanist (with their higher level of morality), the Marcionites (God is a loving, merciful God, but not the God of wrath and justice of the Old Testament. Marcion rewrote the New Testament without mentioning the old Testament). Philo the Alexandrian (Correlated Judaism with Platonism and believed God was unknowable), Valentinos (Gnostic Gospel of Truth), Hermetica (of Egyptian Revelations of Religion and Art). All contributed to force the articulating of the early Christian church beliefs into permanent clear doctrines.

The first three hundred years of the Christian Church, although tumultuous at times, created and recorded the New Testament of the Bible. It did, however, leave it vulnerable to attack from mysticism, rationalism, logic and diverse philosophies. It would be in the next one hundred years that the Church would, in great detail, articulate its beliefs. During this period they did establish five cities with patriarch authority, all of which formed an equal but loose federation. These were Antioch, Jerusalem, Rome, Alexandria and Constantinople. They were said to have been in communion with each other, but did in fact form what was described as a cohesive whole. As we will see later, the Roman Seat slowly but steadily, for the next seven hundred years, gained control or the upper hand, through the introduction of a lineage of Popes, with Papal authority starting at the time of Constantine.

In India, Asceticism becomes a national ideal of the Hindu religion (Accenticism is defined as one that exercises self-denial, especially in spiritual discipline, a hermit). This manifests itself in Yoga. Through Yoga they deny themselves food. They can actually hold their breath for long periods and demonstrate other feats that dominate physical processes. In Yoga they can become one with their God and cut off all sense perceptions. During this time period two great epics were added to the Hindu religion. One was Ramayana a tract on morality and ethics. The other was Mahabharata, which includes one of the most influential Hindu scriptures. It was 600 CE before the next major development.

In 224, the Sassanian Dynasty took the throne of Iran and established Zoroastrianism as the official religion. It also spread through Afghanistan and Persia. One of the religions best recordings were completed, and were called the Avesta. It stresses maintenance of a good life and rejecting evil. After a death the good versus evil is judged. Fault or sins can be forgiven through confession to the saints, because they recognize human frailties. There is no predestination, therefore final determination will rest on the evaluation of good and evil. It was not to become a strong influence after Islam took control in the seventh century. Moving to India they would be called Parses. (or a descendent of the Persian refuges especially in Bombay) They have maintained a strong influence in commerce and in modern times were wealthy, educated and philanthropic.

Chronology of Chapter II

24 CE	Jesus starts ministry.
27	Jesus is crucified.
49	Saul the Jewish Rabbi is converted and called Paul.
64	Mark, earliest of four Gospels is written.
70	Gnostics.
95–110	Revelation is written.
140	Shepherd of Hermas is written that establishes Bishops, Deacons and Priests.
150	Four canonical Gospels are collected.
200	New Testament canon is largely fixed.
200	Didache (Teaching of the twelve Apostles) is written.
240	Heavy persecution of Christians started and lasted through 305 CE.
312	Roman Emperor Constantine the Great converts to Christianity.

3

300–600 CE

❖

Constantine through Augustine

From Constantine through Augustine passed a mere one hundred years, but during this period Christianity became the religion of the State and the Roman Catholic doctrine was definitively recorded with the Nicene Creed. Some will begin this period by stating that it starts with Constantine corrupting the Christian Church and Augustine providing the catalyst which Martin Luther will use after one thousand years of dark ages, to cause the greatest schism of them all. For the Roman Catholics and the Orthodox Catholics this was their starting point and established the saving grace through the trinity. The Catholic Church was faced with constant changes over the centuries. Their Canon became extremely diversified and fluid in nature, with current requirements for social, religious, political, economic and cultural changes.

There was, of course, political history running parallel to the religious struggles. It was during this time that the Romans had their hands full with the Goths from the northern countries of Sweden and West Russia. For one hundred years after Christ they settled on the Black Sea where they learned Christianity. It is very interesting that they had among them a converted Goth who was referred to as a saintly scholar. He conceived and wrote a Gothic alphabet so that he could convert the Christian Bible for his people to read. His name was

Ulfilas. His Bible is historically important because it is claimed to be the oldest for any Teutonic language.

The Goths for a time maintained a great kingdom north of the Danube River and the Black Sea. In 375 CE the Huns swept into Europe from Asia, conquered the East Goths and forced the West Goths across the Danube into Roman boundaries. By 410 CE Rome itself fell to the West Goths (Visigoths). They later gave up Italy in favor of settling a kingdom in France and Spain.

In <u>The History of the Christian Church</u> by Williston Walker, he describes Tertullian (197) as the first writer of prominence to use Latin with a strong influence in this period. Walker devotes fifty pages to the various religious philosophies, which were attacking the Christian doctrine. This period runs from the first general council in 320 which produced the first Nicene Creed and ends with the second council in 381 which wrote the second Nicene Creed, which was eventually rejected in favor of the original Nicene Creed. At the beginning of the third century, several Christologies were competing in Rome. Perhaps the most important was Monasticism, which proclaimed the dispensation of the spirit of the 4th Gospel. This gave rise to the dynamic Monarchians which held that Jesus was the Son of God by adoption and the Modalistic Monarchians claimed that Jesus was the temporary manifestation of One God. This is only a sample, which represents the beginning of the struggle of Christological History before and after the Nicene Creed.

Pre Nicene, the last great influence on Christology was Origen, whose work was often referred to as the greatest intellectual achievement of the anti-Nicene Church. His work was condemned by the Synod of Alexandria in 379, later by Emperor Justinian in 543 and the Fifth General Council in 553.

It is reported that Constantine after becoming Emperor of all of the Roman Empire in 300 was about to go into another battle in which he was outnumbered and outmaneuvered. Legend has it that he saw a cross in the sky, which told him to pray for deliverance, and he decided to resort to prayer to the Christian God to deliver him from his enemy. The martyrdom and longevity of the Christians had impressed him. He won the day and gave the prayer credit for his victory. He was soon converted to Christianity and stopped all the persecutions of the Christians in the Roman Empire.

Constantine soon found himself in the middle of the religious philosophies and disagreements attacking the Church from all sides. The struggle between Gnosticism and Montanism was rampant even as Constantine took command of the Roman Empire in 311 and was converted to Christianity. The Church grew quickly and new laws established churches as corporations, with pay for the leaders. Private heathen sacrifices were prohibited and many churches were built in Rome, Jerusalem, Bethlehem, etc. It was Constantine who first concluded that if you house the church worship in an attractive building the people would be more inclined to come. The icons are another matter as to whether they are a form of idol worship as contended by many or at least a distraction. Much will be said about this later. Most important was that Constantine transferred the capitol to the rebuilt Bysantum, which he called New Rome and was renamed Constantinople. The motive was political and defensive, but was of great consequence. This was the government of the Romans not the Roman Christian Church that moved to Constantinople.

Constantine tried to settle the conflicting views in the Christian Church with a Synod, especially after he discovered Christians persecuting Christians. The followers of Arius claimed Jesus does not share the essence of the Father and were a much greater danger than the barbarians called Goths. Arius was a Presbyter in a Church in Baucalis and disagreed with the Bishop of Alexander over the influence and existence of one God. This was a Monarchian influence in which Christ was One with the Father, Christ was a loving God. Constantine, unable to pacify anyone, had more trouble trying to define the differences among the combatants. He decided to bring the patriarchs, bishops and their staffs together into one big meeting to settle the doctrinal disputes arising from both Aryans and Orthodox. Constantine ordered the council to briefly but definitively produce a statement that would be at least a compromise. Athanasius, Patriarch of Alexander and defender of the Orthodox, persuaded the council to define the divine essence and the absolute equality of the three persons. Thus, the first Nicene Creed was written and documented, but it did not pacify the opponents. There was more bickering and struggle after the Nicene Creed than before it.

On Constantine's death the empire was divided between Constantine II (Britain, Gaul and Spain), Constantius (Asia Minor, Syria and Egypt), Constans, the area in between. Constantine II soon died which caused the empire to be divided between Constans in the West and Constantius in the East. The Nicene controversy continued.

A series of emperors ended with the death of Valens in the Great Roman defeat by the West Goths at Adrianople. Theodosius became emperor, and was the last sole ruler of the Roman Empire. He established the Orthodox Trinitarian Christianity based on the divine Peter the Apostle, mostly in the East.

In 381 Theodosius held an Eastern Synod in Constantinople (2nd General Council), but it did not end the controversy. From the beginning Arian creeds were rejected. The main defender of the Nicene Faith was Athanasius, born in Alexandria in 295 and became the Alexandrian Bishop. The final Nicene theology was due to his effort. Arius was old and died during the debates, it is said because of the stress. In summary, the compromise came about because of the fusion of the Nicene and Semi-Arian or conservative parties.

St. Ambrose, Bishop of Milan, clarified the separation of Church and State, by the end of the fourth century. He taught that the law of the Church could only be administered by the Bishops and even the Emperor was subject to their authority. St. Ambrose was firm and stated "The Emperor is within the Church, not over it." St. Ambrose was, however, intensely loyal to the Emperor.

In the East, after the fall of Rome in 410 CE, the Byzantine Church and State bound together. We are fortunate that this did not happen in the West. Joan O'Grady in <u>Early Christian Heresies</u> points out that from the third century on, there were three Episcopal Sees in the West; Rome, Alexandria and Antioch, of which Rome was preeminent and gained authority over the others. Alexandria was a cosmopolitan center of learning and produced great writers and church leaders. Antioch, on the other hand, had most of their teachers dedicated to morals rather than metaphysical speculation.

By 401 the Visigots were on the march and actually took Rome in 410. An anonymous quote stated that "the old mistress of the world had fallen before the barbarians."

While this was happening, the Saxons and the Jutes increasingly invaded Britain. In Ireland the most popular individual was St. Patrick, formerly a slave for six years. God told him to escape to study for the priesthood and after twelve years he returned to Ireland to spread Christianity. Whether he drove the snakes out of Ireland is a moot question.

The Germanic invaders organized their hold on Italy and made General Odovakak the king in 476. This date is usually taken as the end of the Roman Empire. There were no further Emperors in the West until Charlemagne. Most of the Bishops in Rome kept the authority of the Church but the strongest was Innocent I (402–417) who established universal jurisdiction of Roman Bishops. Leo the First served Rome during the invasion of the Huns and Vandals. He influenced the Council of Chalcedon and emphasized the primacy of Peter among the Apostles in church affairs and government. Innocent and Leo no doubt both felt that in order to permanently establish the Roman authority over the other patriarchs, they would have to create an individual with a strong hand (a Pope). They chose Peter and used a passage in the Bible to prove his individual authority over the church. Only the Catholics hold Peter in such high esteem. Paul would have been a more likely choice as the image on which the Pope is defined, due in part to the very existence of gentiles in the church and his overall influence in creating the Christian Church.

By far the most significant contribution to religious dogma and history was St. Augustine, the fourth century Bishop of Hippo. For nine years he was associated with Manicheism, but later found that it was a cosmic myth. He has been referred to as the Father of Western Theology or the greatest of the Latin Church fathers. Historians agree that no other theologian except Paul has influenced the Church more. St. Augustine was a teacher in Rome before he and his son (by a former mistress), were baptized by St. Ambrose in 386. He became bishop of Hippo in 396, and became a leader of orthodoxy. He wrote a large volume of work, of which the most important were the twenty-two books called the City of God. In these books he describes the City of God as connected to the earth through the Church. Much of the Church doctrine was created or interpreted by him, although it would be in serious theological dispute with later Protestantism. David W. Bercot, in his book <u>Will the Real Heretics Please Stand Up</u>, makes a list of what he considers the most important contribution, but by no means a conclusive list of the controversial contributions by Augustine, as follows:

That Mary was born and lived her entire life without actual sin.
That unbaptized infants are eternally damned.
That war can be holy.
That there is no forgiveness of sins outside the Catholic Church.
That some of the practices and teachings of the Apostles no longer apply to Christians because the Apostles lived in a different age.
That there is a purgatorial fire.
That the dead can benefit from the sacrifice of the Eucharist.
That it is proper for a Christian State to persecute heretics.

It is obvious that St. Augustine had his distractions, even as he was formulating the above. One such opponent was Pelagius, a Monk from Britain in 400 CE, who argued that individuals could live sinless and thereby save themselves. St. Augustine contended that salvation is totally a matter of grace, but many feel that he possibly went too far in proving his point, and drifted from the teachings of the early Christians. David Bercot in <u>Real Heretics</u> states "in the place of free will and man's involvement of salvation, Augustine substituted a cold, grim doctrine of predestination." Joan O' Grady in <u>Christian Heresies</u> explains that Pelagius would not agree that Adam's sin could condemn the whole human race, that unbaptized infants were automatically damned, that the human race does not die because of Adam, nor rise again because of Christ alone. St. Augustine is said to have argued with Pelagius to such an extent that he developed his counter arguments into intolerable harshness. The struggle was basically about original sin. Pelagius taught that mankind was not redeemed in its entirely through baptism. He gave ethics the main emphasis. There is no universality of sin and there is no universality of salvation. Grace could come to any person at any time. It is interesting to note that in the years to follow, before the days of Martin Luther, that the sides will switch. This is because of a pragmatic need to raise money to build the cathedrals in Rome by selling indulgences, which contradicts the theory of predestination. It implies that man can therefore help himself. In the reformation it is Martin Luther who is preaching predestination.

To summarize the Church Ecumenical Councils is at best difficult because of the serious complicated doctrines being discussed. The first council at Nicene in what is now Turkey, in 325, was assembled mostly to settle the dispute between Arius from Alexandria and Athanasius, assistant to the bishop of Alexandria. The name Arius today is synonymous with heresy, but even Origen earlier had discussed these views. The question was how could Jesus Christ have been God, the same as God the Father. The outcome was the Nicene Creed, and the Trinity was established, but the conflict went on for several hundred years.

The second Council in 390 ratified biblical canon at Constantinople. The Nicene Creed was made the definition of Christian orthodoxy, and the church was declared Trinitarian (Father, Son and Holy Ghost). It was the eastern part of the empire fighting to maintain these doctrines because the west was too busy with their struggle with barbarians. During the fourth and fifth century they were growing further apart and would be known as the Latin West and the Greek East. Their liturgy was beginning to differ.

The 3rd council general of Ephesus in 431 was a conflict created by Nestorius, when he declared no one should call the Virgin Mary the Mother of God, but should say Mother of Jesus. Palagius who taught that man could live without sin was condemned, but Palagius persisted that Adam did not establish sin for all mankind, that baptism was not necessary to forgive the sins of Adam. He felt man can live a righteous life on his own. The whole struggle was over original sin and the two persons in Christ. There was no consensus and the debate carried on.

The 4th council in 451 was held in Chalcedon. They debated the "Tomb of Leo," which was a restatement of the Nicene Creed which was to guard against Monophysitism and Nestorianism, both of which had condemned the Tomb of Leo, and it was approved mostly by the Eastern church representatives. Despite this agreement the fight continued. Athanasius denied that the Virgin Mary could be called the Mother of God and defended the doctrine of two persons (one human and one divine). The "Tomb of Leo" was accepted as Christology.

The 5th council was in Ephesus, called the robber council, which ended in turmoil and was dissolved.

The 6th council was held in 680. The eastern part of the Roman Empire settled the doctrine of the divine will in Christ and Monophysitism was finally contained. The settlement was not so much an agreement on dogma or orthodoxy, but because they had to defend the Islam onslaught. The use of icons because of western influence was limited to veneration (respect).

Only the Eastern Church attended the 7th council in Constantinople in 787. They approved the use of icons in worship, which was referred to as finally settling the iconoclastic controversy. The Roman Church remained at only veneration (respect) for icons.

After Constantine and even more so after St. Augustine, a very different church evolved. The first change was that church buildings sprang up in the leading Christian areas. Secondly, the leaders were free to go out into the world to spread the Word. Thirdly, anyone who disagreed with the established Christian doctrine was declared heretic and could be burned at the stake.

During this period through 450 CE, the religious laws of Hinduism were completed or at least added to. The caste system proliferated. The triad, Brahma, Vishnu and Shiva, were the main catalysts of their religion but there were many lesser Gods. There was an impetus for Theistic Schools of Theology.

Jainism continued in India and is still active today. It is characterized by the absolute fanatic protection of all living creatures. It was in reaction to the old sacrificing of animals and developed to a point of sweeping the streets before you walked on them so that you would not crush a living organism. It was carried so far as to not wash yourself to keep from killing body lice. Jains may not take a job where weapons or alcohol are manufactured or used.

During this period a traveler or pilgrim from China named Fa-Hsien, studied in India and brought back to China books and manuscripts, which brought Buddhism to China, The World's Great Religions however, gives the most final credit for bringing Buddhism to China to Hsuan-Tsang in 629 CE. Trade between India, China and the West brought many travelers in the third and fourth century. Buddhist scholars were discussing or debating with the Confucius, Taoist, Zoroastrians, Manichaeans and Nestorian Christians, which proved, at least for China, that Buddhism was the most pertinent of them all. Mahayana Buddhism proved to be the most popular or accepted of the Buddhist doctrines in China. It was divided into three groups, the Shin Sect being noted for pageants and celebrations, one of which is a very large celebration conducted yearly for Buddha's birthday. Shin-Shu was the most powerful of the three. Its priests marry and often pass their office on to their sons. It has the greatest number of temples, monks and teachers. Zen is the second largest with stern discipline. They believe in plain living and long years of meditation, referred to as the noblest branch. They believe that if meditation is conducted properly that in time it will bring a flash of enlightenment. Buddhism up to this time was scholastic in nature. The Buddhist monks in the temples and monasteries had their codes and morality standards, but lacked the pragmatic application of the early Buddhist philosophies. It was the introduction of Zen that brought serious consideration to morality.

Buddhism like Existentialism teaches self-help and self-reliance as the most important path to Nirvana. It does include mutual help, universal services and brotherhood. It has been explained as a religion without God and as purely humanistic, which is dedicated or devoted to liberation of the suffering man. It is best described as the eight-fold way to perfect peace and tranquility. It also includes the removal of ignorance, which would lead to Nirvana. Right understanding, right thought, right speech, right action, right livelihood, right effort, right mindfulness, and right concentration. In addition, the four noble truths became part of the very essence of Buddhism. Noble truth concerning the nature of suffering, the noble truth concerning the origin of suffering, noble truth concerning removal of suffering, realization of Nirvana, and the truth concerning the path leading to the removal of suffering. Through these truths suffering is seen to be everywhere, but it can be prevented and removed. One definition that can cover the three major religions in India is that each defines Liberation or Salvation as a state of mind. This is not to be achieved after death but in this very life. Each individual can achieve his goal in life. In Hindu this is called Moksha, in Jains Kaivalya, in Buddha it's Nirvana.

In Judaism, like all religions, documentation was still taking place. Around 200 CE, Rabbi Judah assembled an important collection of Rabbinical Laws, in what is called the Mishnah. Jewish scholars into what is called the very authoritative and influential Talmud in 500 CE, however, combined this with studies and laws. This spelled out the laws covering many Jewish traditions such as worship, social responsibility, and even health.

Chronology of Chapter III

312	Roman Emperor Constantine converts to Christianity following a vision.
313	Constantine grants legal rights to Christians, returns confiscated property.
330	Constantine moves the capital to Constantinople.
350	Brothers Vasubandhu and Asanga start the second school of Mayhayana Buddhism.
372	Buddhism spreads to Korea.
375	Sacred texts by Puranas of Hindu Gods Brahama, Vishnu, and Shiva.
376	Earliest listing of the New Testament Canon in its present form.
387	Augustine converts to Christianity, writes the influential <u>City of God</u>.
395	Roman Empire is split between Eastern and Western Empires.
400	Anglo-Saxon pagans obliterate Christianity in England.
405	Jerome completes the Vulgate, which is the Roman Catholic Latin Bible.
418	British Monk Pelagius denies original sin and need for baptism, defeated by Augustine.
430	St. Patrick brings Christianity to Ireland.
451	Council of Ephesus declares Mary is Mother of God and Christ.
476	Roman Empire collapses, but western church leaders remain in Rome.
530	The largest church structure, the Hagia Sofia, is built in Constantinople, later taken over by Islam.

Definition of Second, Third and Fourth Century Groups With Religious Ideas Conflicting With The Nicene Creed

GNOSTICISM: Greek for knowledge, a belief that salvation comes from an insight secret knowledge, the capacity to discover truths by the help of your intellect alone. Recognized for its dualism, everything is the result of a fight between two powers or two qualities, the good and the evil. Valentinus was a main disciple.

MANICHAEISM: Founded in Persia by Mani who promoted and was a believer in a syncretistic religion (a combination of different forms of faiths) He taught the release of the spirit through asceticism (a hermit). A semi-Gnostic.

ASCETICISM: A hermit practicing strict self-denial as a measure of personal and spiritual discipline.

DONATISTS: Sacraments by the unworthy were invalid. No Priest without sanctity could dispense the Eucharist and Baptism.

MARCIONITE: Antagonism to the Old Testament. Many were converts to Manicheism by the third century. They wrote a New Testament with no mention of the Old Testament.

MONTANISM: Christian movement derived from Mantanus of Phrygia, and two women, Prisca and Maximilla, whose expectation was that the end of the world was at hand. They had a wide following. It was austere, ethical and spiritual, but was opposed by the Catholic Church. The Bishops in Asia Minor excommunicated them and they did not survive.

MONOPHYSITE: They believed that God had only one nature which was divine and not human. In the Chalcedon Council it was agreed that Christ has two natures, human and divine. Monophysites rejected this but were condemned in the third Council. In later centuries this influenced, particularly, the Armenian, Coptic and Eastern Churches.

ARIANISM: Developed by the Priest Arius, who started a dispute with his Bishop Alexander by claiming that Jesus does not share the essence with the Father, or is dissimilar with the Father. Jesus is more than man but less than God.

PELAGIANISM: Developed by Pelagius, the theologian. Human nature is basically good and the people are free to choose between right and wrong. Sin is a voluntary act. He denied the doctrine of original sin and the need for baptism.

MONASTICISM: Form of religious life found in both Roman Orthodox and Buddhism. Perfection is achieved through solitary ascetic existence with voluntary poverty (whole or partial seclusion from the secular world). Life of devotion and worship. The Rule of Benedict was the most significant of the early monastic life.

MONARCHIANS: (Modalistic) They held that Christ was a temporary form of manifestation of the one God. They defined Father, Son and Holy Ghost as one God, which ultimately through Augustine, triumphs.

MONARCHIANS: (Dynamic) Jesus was the Son of God by adoption, one of the oldest concepts in Christology, as an impersonal attribute of the Father. By this Jesus was united by love to God but did not become a substitute for God.

4

500–900 CE

❖

Islam

By far the most significant development in this period was the rise of the Arab Prophet Mohammed, 570–632 CE. He was born in Mecca, the son of a not too successful merchant. His father and his mother both died when he was only six years old. He was raised by an uncle and a grandfather and was married quite young, with six children resulting from this marriage. One of his daughters was married to the 3rd Caliph. (Emperor) At the age of thirty he started getting revelations of the word of God, who he called Allah.

His revelations called for the destruction of idols, to give gifts to the poor and care for the orphans. These caused a great deal of hostility in Mecca, a city not only a commerce center but also a religious center with many different forms of idol worship. A shrine common to all of the religious forms was the Kaaba. The opposition, mostly Jews, and actual threats, caused him and a small group to flee and to build up a following in a more receptive area. He would later come back to Mecca with ten thousand men and take the area by force. By 630 he controlled all of Arabia.

The debate still goes on as to whether he was illiterate, and as a result did not write the Koran (Muslim Bible), which contains all his revelations. It seems strange but his followers want him to be illiterate so that all his revelations would have come directly from God. The question of illiteracy becomes confusing, considering that his grandfather Adu Talib taught the young Mohammed to be a merchant, which would most likely have included both writing and reading to manage the paper work. This, however, seems to be a moot point as to the intellectual acumen of the prophet. His revelations over twenty years came from God, and like Jesus and Buddha, he just didn't subject the doctrines to writing. He, like the others, left an extensive oral path to the Koran, as Jesus did the Bible, and Buddha did the Pali-Canon. During the rule of the third Caliph the revelations were put in book form with 114 chapters arranged by chapter length.

The Jews and the Muslims both agree that there is one God and only one God, who was the God of Abraham. Both the Jews and the Muslims claim descendency from Abraham depending on which side of the biblical story is taken as substantiation. The story in the Old Testament starts with Abraham's wife Sarah, who couldn't conceive and produce a son for Abraham. In what must have been desperation, she suggested to her husband that he should take her maid or slave girl to produce a son. The slave girl had a son by Abraham and called him Ismael. Soon after, Sarah however, became pregnant and had a son whom she called Isaac. Sarah now had a problem in that she didn't want Ismael and the slave girl in their household. Abraham apparently loved them both, but now the difference in interpretation presents itself. According to the Jews it was Isaac who was taken to the mountain top to become a human sacrifice to prove Abraham loved God above all else. God stopped the process by calling out to Abraham not to light the fire, that he had proven his devotion. The Jews are descendents of Isaac. The Islam translation is that it was Ismael who went to the mountain with his father. The Muslims therefore, claim to be descendent from Ismael.

The Muslim rules of conduct are contained in the Koran, but the explanation of the words and deeds of Mohammed are contained in the Sharia (meaning the right path). This is a code of law that regulates all Muslims. The Koran is God given. The Sharia is man made. Unfortunately it does not cover everything and is used or interpreted differently by different groups or states. There is some confusion caused by the fact that Mohammed only ruled on current events and as history changed, new situations required new rules, which were then added to the Sharia.

As contrasted to St. Augustine, who declared that war can be holy, Muslims especially the Shiites, believed war of conquest can not only be holy, but one who dies in the pursuit will inherit heaven, with no evaluation of previous sins. This is where the Muslim world is always in conflict with other nations and religions, because Islam felt they were obligated to conquer the world. Their armies in one hundred years took territory from India in the east to Spain in the west.

Islam has no separation between church and state, but all acknowledge that the role of Mohammed is that of the messenger who established the five pillars of Muslim.

1875	Profession of Faith (Shahada)
1876	Daily Prayer
1877	Gifts to the Poor—Alms Tax
1878	Fasting in the month of Ramadan
1879	Pilgrimage to Mecca

These are considered obligations and/or instructions for the faith. Five daily prayers are a compromise in number from two to forty as originally suggested. Congregational prayer is required only on Friday noon and some holidays.

One interesting aspect of Muslim prayer in the sanctuary is what is called Rakatin. It is a series of bends, from the waist, on the knees erect, and down with the forehead on the floor. This is what introduces the prayer blankets. In the Mosque they line up so that they don't touch each other in the various bends. Women usually pray in separate areas. From my personal experience in Bangladesh, on a Friday at 11:00 a.m., I was returned to my hotel so that my associates could go to the Mosque, I observed that the poor people or common folks didn't go to the Mosque. The streets were just as crowded as before, so I used this time to go by rickshaw to the famous Bangli Gangi River, to sightsee and take pictures.

After Mohammed, the new rulers, called Caliphs, would argue for generations, as to who would lead. Like all Islam dynasties, they are sure to change. No system or rules for the selection of future rulers or Caliphs was ever established by Mohammed. (The Shiites still believe he did).

The first Caliph selected by associates of Mohammed, was Abu Bakr, to be defender of the faith. The selection was made in lieu of Ali, Mohammed's son-in-law, and would result in conflicting views of the authenticity of the selection process.

Umar succeeded Abu Bakr during a period of Muslim army success, the overpowering of all of the Arabian Peninsula. The Islamic military success was not entirely military skill, but was at least aided by the pre-existence of discontent in the absorbed territory. This was due in part by the fact that the Muslim religion was not forced on them and they conducted their day to day lives pretty much as before. It is reported that in most cases the army was barracked in a separate area in order to cause less imposition on the conquered.

Umar served as Caliph for ten years and was assassinated by a disgruntled slave. No one would ever have the support and hold the various units together and gain as much as Umar. The third Caliph was Uthman, who had been a friend of Mohammed. He was not a strong leader but did have an official compilation of the Koran made so as to stop false doctrines from filtering into the faith. Finally the elders of Medina made Ali, Mohammed's son-in-law, the Caliph, but he was weak and had to protect his position by being the first Muslim to fight Muslims. These four are the last to know Mohammed and soon after Ali was assassinated, the Umayyad Dynasty took control and lasted for over a century. During this time the Empire grew to its furthest points. Only Constantinople held out against the Islam onslaught.

Marwan II, the last Umayyad Caliph, was defeated in 750, and the Caliph position was passed to Abbasids. The long reign of the Umayyads was over and the Abbasids brought the zenith of Islamic civilization. They moved the capital to Iraq.

In his book, <u>Understanding Islam</u>, Thomas Lipman states that while Europe was passing through the dark ages, the Abbasid Empire established itself as the custodian of civilization, where ancient traditions of science and philosophy were preserved. Works in Greek, Syrian, Sanskrit, and Persian, were saved from oblivion by being translated into Arabic. Innovations such as the decimal system were created. Great strides were made in art, medicine, mathematics, poetry and architecture. The most prominent architecture is the Christian shrine at Cordoba, Spain. It was built as a Muslim Mosque and later changed to a Christian Cathedral, a masterpiece on any scale. It should also be noted that Ireland also saved much of the ancient traditions in science, literature and religious material. This was the literature in the libraries that the barbarians were burning in Europe.

Baghdad was the World Center of culture and science, but the fragmenting of the empire was beginning. The local Persian dynasty called the Buwaihids, took over the capital in 945 and remained to control the Abbasid Caliphs for the next century.

Still within this time period, was the creation of the Fatimids, an independent Shiite dynasty, out of Tunisia, who claimed decendency from Ali, (one of Mohammed's son-in-laws) and took command over North Africa, including Egypt. They founded Al-Qahiram (Cairo in English) to replace Baghdad as the center of Islamic culture and learning. They also established the Al-Azhar Mosque, which is still the center of Muslim and Arab scholarship.

Political stability or Muslim cohesiveness was not to be. One dynasty after another robbed them of a great empire. It must also be kept in mind that not all Muslims are Arabs. Thomas Lippman's <u>Understanding Islam</u> indicates that "Islam continued to expand into new corners of the world, propagated not by marching armies or

Caliphate will, but by osmosis, by human contact, commerce, and example. That process is a testimony to Islam's appeal to people of many cultures."

Further fragmenting and decline resulted from outside invasion. One of these was the famous Genghis Khan and his grandson Hulegu, brother of Kubla Kahn. The pagan Mongols swept through what is now Turkey, Iraq and Iran. They stormed Baghdad and the Abbasid Caliph surrendered after a siege. It's best I quote from Arthur Goldschmidt's <u>Concise History of the Middle East</u>. "The Mongols pillaged the city, burned its schools and libraries, destroyed its Mosques and Palaces, murdered a million Muslims (the Christians and Jews were spared), and finally executed the whole Abbasid family by wrapping them in carpets and trampling them beneath their horses hooves. Until the stench of the dead forced Hulegu and his men from Baghdad, they loaded their horses, packed the scabbards of their discarded swords and even stuffed some gutted corpses with gold, pearls and precious stones to be hauled back to the Mongol capital. It was a tragic end to the independent Abbasid Caliphate, to the prosperity and intellectual glory of Baghdad and for some historians, to Arabic civilization itself."

The Hulegu destruction of Baghdad was a severe blow but the center of Islam was already in Cairo. Even more important, the Muslim religion had become international. The seat of Islam in Cairo was not controlled by Arabians or Egyptians, but a force of Turks and Persians who were former slave soldiers called Mamelukes. They were good soldiers and Muslims who when Hulegu sent word that Cairo was next and that they should surrender, they killed the envoys and set out to meet the Mongols in Palestine. Much to the Mongols surprise they were defeated by the force of Islam and driven out. The empire of Islamic Arabs was now only part of history. Some of the descendants of the Mongols settled in Persia and adopted Islam in the thirteenth century.

It is interesting to note that Muslims controlled Jerusalem for thirteen centuries. There is no mention of Jerusalem in the Koran. Muslims at one time faced Jerusalem to pray but later changed to Mecca.

In other areas, during this time period, Zoroastrians survived through the Islamic spread, but were forced to move to India, even though there were a few left in Iran.

Korean missionaries spread Buddhism to Japan. By 650, the Buddha monks were sent by the Japanese government to convert or teach in the remote areas. In my research it seemed strange how many sects grew out of Buddhism, but why should we wonder at these aspects when we look at Protestantism which has divided into thousands of denominations.

Confucianism was being taught in schools by this time, but it had its ups and downs depending on the dynasty at the time.

India is more complicated and I find a blur of definitions in the various theological groups. The Rg-Veda is one of the four books and the most important, which made up the Vedas (very old ancient text) which contains very old hymns with traces of mysticism and asceticism, which in the sixth century BCE developed into the Upanishad. This was a text in prose, which gave way to verse or verse mixed with prose. Out of the principles of ancient lore, the Mahabharata completed in 500 CE appears to be the most important and reflects later doctrine. It must be kept in mind that Europe was in the dark ages while India was a country of highest human progress, evolution and civilization.

In <u>Classical Hinduism</u>, by Basham, it is reported that the Mahabharta was finally edited in 500 CE. Traditionally it was believed to be authored by the Sage Krsna Vyasa, apparently it was recited orally to students. The Mahabharata began as poems but was converted to religious texts, which is basically a history lesson. Much of the early Pali scriptures of the Buddhists, long after his death, agree with this text. The most important Gods are Brahma and Indra, but it can be noted that none of the Gods are omnipotent. Again from Basham, Brahma was here recognized as the guardian of the world. Indra ruled the lower heavens and looked on as a rainmaker rather than a war God. The other Gods of the Vedic Pantheon are still important. Vishnu gained popularity but Shiva is in a minor role. Samsana (circle of rebirth) continued, as did Ahimsa (non-violence). Yoga continues to be the most important form of meditation.

To complicate matters there was a second epic Ramayana, which was older than the first, but which I have dismissed in my research because its chronology claims stories told 870,000 years ago. It is called the primeval poem for just that reason. Geology and history would disprove this epic.

The Krishna is another group dedicated to Asceticism, which is extreme self-denial and fasting for spiritual achievement. Even through modern times, their spiritual advancement is through vegetarianism, no use of alcohol, no gambling, and they are celibate except for procreation in marriage. The original Krishna (Krsna) was the eighth incarnation in human form of the deity Vishnu, as told in the Mahabharata. Their original concept was begging for food and experiencing near starvation. If they do die of malnutrition it was rewarded in some kind of spiritual victory, which is difficult to understand.

Chronology of Chapter IV

600	Pope Gregory the Great initiates reform in liturgy and administration. Increases the power of the Pope.
632	Mohammed died.
634	Muslims conquer Syria, Iraq, Egypt and Persia.
656	Through 661 Ali (Mohammed's son-in-law) rules as 4th Caliph.
661	Through 680 Umayyad Dynasty is formed and has it's capital in Damascus.
709	Muslin conquest of Spain begins.
726	Emperor Leo III begins icon controversy between east and west by banning religious icons.
750	Muslim dynasty Abbasid starts after the defeat of Umayyad Caliph, capital in Iraq.
732	Muslims are stopped at Poiter in France.
800	Charlemagne was crowned Emperor by Pope Leo III, creating a new relationship between Church and State. Emperor's authority depends on the Pope.
843	Worship of icons is restored in the east by Michael III.
910	Shiites conquer North Africa.
988	Vladimir I, Grand Duke of Kiev declares Eastern Orthodox Christianity state religion of Russia.

5

700–800 CE

❖

Charlemagne

As early as the sixth century the Roman Empire was showing serious differences between the Greek East and the Latin West. The liturgy was even changing and after 787, icons became important in the whole liturgical aura in the East. The 796 synod of western bishops met in France to insert an extra clause into the Nicene Creed. This explained or stated that the holy spirit proceeded not only from the Father but also from the Son (called the Filioque). This was to emphasize the equality of the Father and of the Son. The Greeks felt that the Latins made the trinity too comprehensible and that the Latin language was not able to express these Trinitarian ideas with sufficient precision. The addition of the Filioque made the Trinity too rational. They might have settled their differences, if fighting invaders had not taken up so much of their time, but the schism was permanent when the crusade sacked Constantinople.

In the west the invading barbarians success was due in part to the political and economic problems of the Roman Empire, which fell as the Goths, Vandals, Lombards, Franks, Angels, Saxons, and others, sacked the Empire. St. Jerome wrote, "the whole world is sinking into ruin." This is because the invaders, with their rude barbarian ways, replaced the organized rules of law and government, which were referred to as the "Dark Ages."

Of the barbarians, only the Franks established a permanent state in Gaul (France). Clovis, their first leader, gained the support of the Roman Catholic Pope. The Church Monks living in monasteries began bringing out the knowledge of the Roman arts and industries. Christianity would bring Europe out of the dark ages. Furthermore, they started the cultural foundation for the middle ages.

It was Charles Martel, leader of the Franks, who finally stopped the Islamic onslaught that had penetrated Europe via Spain. Islam felt compelled to spread the word of Mohammed by capturing the whole world, and they almost did. It is amazing that their conquest covered much of Central Asia, Persia, Mesopotamia, the Arabian Peninsula, North Africa and Spain. It was the Battle of Tours in 732, where the Frank's Charles Martel stopped them. The fate of Europe hung in the balance. It was up to Martel, who was leading a force of French barbarians. The battle was won and he not only defeated the Muslims, but also soon after drove them out of France. Charles never became King, but faced many invaders, such as the Saxons, Bavarians, Allemanni, and the other Germanic tribes. He established a permanent kingdom and was converted to Christianity. He and his son Pippin spread Christianity while assisting St. Boniface. Pippin, who had gained the French throne, had a famous son, Charlemagne, who became King of France in 768.

Charlemagne fought Barbarians and finally the Anglo Saxons, which made him ruler of Europe. For his successful spreading of Christianity, in the year 800 on Christmas Day, the Pope crowned him "Holy Roman Emperor." One of his significant contributions was the reawakening of the arts, law and order, political rights and culture. Compton's Encyclopedia described him as sympathetic to peasants, a fair arbitrator, but a forceful Emperor. He personally inspected the various areas of his broad Kingdom for laxity in government. He tried to drive out the Islamic forces in Spain, but they drove him back into France. When the Roman Church decided to confirm the Filioque in the Nicene Creed, Charlemagne supported the Pope who considered it as Canon.

After Charlemagne, the European situation grew into feudalism. There were innumerable raiding bands of Vikings near the seas and rivers, plus marauding bands of barbarians, to steal and plunder the area. In order to gain support, the King allotted land to overlords for the promise of military support, and to supply an army. People gathered near the castle of a land overseer for protection. The peasants were forced to work a required number of days in the landlord's fields and had to pay taxes to him. In addition they were required to pay a tithe or ten percent to the Church. If he finished working his Lord's field and raised chickens, then every tenth chicken went to the Church. They faced the forces of nature, such as plagues, cold, floods, plus the warfare that ravaged the countryside. Compton explains, however, that they may not have been any worse off than today's poor. They participated in the Church festivals and all the Church holidays, if they could stay alive until the next one.

In the Byzantine era, 337–453, the Roman Empire had fallen, but not the Roman Pope and the seat of the Western Roman Church. Constantinople housed the heads of the Eastern Church, who were called Patriarchs. Compton suggests the Eastern Church golden age was 527 to 565, during Justinian's reign. He built churches, palaces and public areas. They were soon faced with the Islam onslaught, which took the majority of their territory, reducing the eastern section of Christianity to what is now Turkey.

Controversy continues concerning Monophysitism, and religious doctrinal differences continue until the permanent schism or split in 1054, forever dividing Roman Catholicism and Orthodox Catholicism. The word Catholic means Christian, and the word Orthodox means Original. So historically, what is the Orthodox Church? The book by Frank Schaeffer <u>Dancing Alone</u>, the quest for Orthodox faith in the age of false religion tells of the author's conversion from Presbyterianism to the Greek Orthodox Church. He makes many good points on the beauty of the Church, and the deterioration of religion, but historically, the Eastern section of the Christian church is not any more original than the west or the Roman section. We have discussed that there were five equal Patriarchs in Christianity, which were located in Antioch, Alexandria, Jerusalem, Rome and Constantinople. Each made important contributions to the Christian Church, and each provided individuals of varying theological views. The Persians and the Arabs captured Antioch, Alexandria and Jerusalem. Other extraneous circumstances, therefore, rather than religious philosophy, contributed to the Church being split into East and West. The Greek term for original doesn't seem to fit the situation, when you consider that the Nicene Creed wasn't even written until 340 CE, and then it was fought over for another two hundred years. The East changed the Icon situation in 787.

The modern day Amish will tell you that the original religion can only be based on the early Christians, such as Polycarp, Irenaeus, Justine, etc., all in the first two hundred years after the death of Christ. Another interesting fact on the original Church concept comes from our organ tuner, who maintains that the original Christians met in each other's homes. He and other believers take turns having Church meetings to discuss the Bible and to pray. They truly believe that ornate buildings distract from direct communication with God. It was Constantine's view that a solemn house dedicated to God in any religion will attract people.

Hinduism also made changes in this time period. Included in the Mahabharta is the Bhagavad-Gita, the most important and influential religious text in India, and also the best known. Translated it means "Sung by the Lord." It contains important passages and messages from modern Hinduism. The trend toward Theism was becoming a dominant force. Krsna was loved, which was a demonstration of devotion to God. The devotee, according to Basham, was performing Bhakti, a form of religious practice suggested in the Bhagavad-Gita. Salvation by means of devotion was now open to all humans regardless of birth, gender or station in life. This was called the Grupa period, and resulted in the construction of permanent structures or temples. It is interesting to note that this is the same time period that Christian churches were being built. The leaders of the Grupa dynasty were followers of Hinduism, and their symbol was Visnu. Theism became a state religion. Temples became the repositories of wealth, religious art and textbooks. During this time, Hinduism was changing into a modern religion.

Another important historical fact during this period was the conversion of Russia to the Greek Orthodox Church as a state religion. It must be noted that the Russian Church is for all intents and purposes the Greek Church, but unfortunately there are no official ties similar to those of the Pope of the Roman Church. This has resulted in a problem for the Orthodox Churches because they don't have common leadership for growth, such as the Popes in Rome.

6

1096–1270 (1492)

❖

Crusades

The crusades represent a most significant and disastrous period of church history, which most accounts limit to the crusades in the Holy Land 1096–1270. In reality there were church sponsored crusades from 1300 to 1492, to various European areas. It is true that the first and most obvious goal was to free the Holy Land, which in the end they failed to do. Other influences and results came about through greed, adventure and a search for new frontiers. It was all made possible when the Pope instituted a form of creative financing through the doctrine of indulgences. If a knight or foot soldier signed up for a crusade, all his previous sins would be forgiven. This is to set the stage for the reformation over 400 years later, because indulgences were soon to be expanded to other areas where the Roman Church needed money.

It all got started when the Turks defeated the Saracens. When the Saracens (desert people) held Jerusalem, Christians had for many years made pilgrimages to visit their most holy places, the tomb of Christ, the places where Jesus walked and died. When the Turks controlled Jerusalem, the tourists were harassed, robbed, and some killed. When these atrocities were reported in the East, fear of the Turks caused the Emperor of the eastern church, Alexius Commenus, to beg the Roman church, Pope Urban II, for protection and aid to protect Constantinople.

The Council of Clement was held in France in 1095. Compton Encyclopedia refers to the Pope's speech as eloquent and historically has never been surpassed in greater results. Fired with religious zeal to free the Holy Land, the clergy, knights, and common people shouted "God Wills It."

The first crusade 1096 to 1099, with the battle cry "God Wills It," was assembled in great haste and anticipation of victory. Two bands or units couldn't wait. One band of several thousand, under a knight called Walter the Penniless (that may imply he didn't have much money and felt the crusades would offer financial gain), but living off the countryside didn't work. The Turks east of Constantinople massacred his hungry army in ambush. The other poorly conceived band of thousands was under the command of a Monk named Peter the Hermit. He probably should have stayed a hermit because over half of his army died and the balance became slaves.

An unfortunate result of forming the first crusade was the first holocaust. Crusaders killed Jews by the thousands and confiscated their belongings. The Jews were not impressed with the Pope's indulgences and resisted cash donations. The killing of Jews was evident on several occasions before the crusades were over. From 1290 to 1500, the Jews were denied land and forced into the ghettos. In 1290 they were expelled from England, from France in 1392, from Spain in 1492, and from Portugal in 1407. Many of the German Jews escaped from Germany into Poland.

The real forces of the first crusade finally assembled in 1096. The leaders were Godfrey of Bouillon, Robert of Normandy, Richard of Toulouse, and Bohemond the Norman. They created the Red Cross, not to be confused with the present Red Cross, to sew on their tunics, which they wore on the front of their uniforms going to the Holy Land and on their backs upon returning. With great anticipation they set off for the Holy Land, and took seven months attempting to capture Antioch (City of Great Towers). The Turks finally were driven out but the situation reversed itself when the Turks attacked the Christians now in

Antioch. Disease and starvation soon cut their forces and their enthusiasm. It was the Priest Peter Bartholomew who came up with the clever revelation, in which he had dreamed that the spearhead that had pierced Jesus' side could be found under the alter of the church. He, of course, found the spearhead, which was to be a sign from heaven that they would be successful in capturing Jerusalem. With new determination they broke out of Antioch after six months when it was evident that the Turks had been fighting among themselves and part of their army had left the assault. The crusaders pushed on to Jerusalem, where they took Jerusalem in several weeks, with only a few thousand of the original force of tens of thousands. According to Compton the Christian crusaders after capturing Jerusalem on 15 July 1099, shamefully massacred the defeated Turks.

Some of the crusaders that were left returned to their homes and the force that was to remain in Jerusalem made Godfrey of Bouillon ruler. They built castles for a permanent stay. They even created three special orders of knighthood. The Knights Hospitallers grew out of helping the sick and wounded crusaders. The Knights Templars received their name from their location in the Temple of Solomon in Jerusalem. The Teutonic Knights were created later but all three became involved with political and economic matters as well as military. After building hospitals and garrisons around Palestine, they created branches back home. Kings gave them land and power so their influence grew. They are important to religious history because they were called to attend church councils.

When Muslim power spread in the Holy Land, Louis VII of France and Conrad III of Germany assembled the second crusade. It is reported that confusion and mismanagement caused the second crusade to experience failure. The Muslim ruler Saladin had seized Jerusalem. He was kind to his captives, even allowing some of them to go home and some to be ransomed. He didn't massacre the defeated foe as the first crusade had done.

The third crusade, 1189 to 1191, was to drive Saladin, the Muslim ruler, out of Jerusalem. The leaders were Richard the Lion Hearted of England, Philip Augustis of France, and the much older Emperor of Germany, Frederick Barbarossa. The expedition was altered when Barbarossa drowned in Asia Minor. Richard and Philip took their armies by sea where they joined Christians besieging Acre (a seaport 109 miles from Haifa). It was apparently necessary to capture the city of Acre to progress on to Jerusalem via Haifa (the largest seaport in what is now Israel). It was in Haifa as well as Jerusalem that the first crusaders slaughtered Arabs and Jews alike. It took twenty-three months to capture Acre. By this time Philip and Richard were quarreling so Philip went home to France. Unfortunately, Richard never took Jerusalem, losing thousands of his men, but did make a three-year truce with Saladin, to allow Christians to make pilgrimages to the Holy Land. Saladin, who according to Compton, was the most famous of Muslim military heroes, having captured Egypt, Syria, Palestine and North Mesopotamia

Richard had two enemies in Europe, Philip of France, his former partner in the Crusades, and Leopold, Duke of Austria. His army had been reduced to a few knights, so for his trip home, he had to go in disguise. It didn't work and he was captured when someone betrayed him. He was taken prisoner and was held until his brother raised the money back in England, to bail him out of captivity. He was a different kind of King in that he never stayed home. In England he raised money to go back to Europe to fight the French.

The Fourth Crusade, 1202 to 1204, was planned to attack the Muslims in Egypt by crossing the Mediterranean Sea. The crusaders couldn't come up with the money to pay the Venetians for the ships so the Venetians came up with a scheme to finance the ships in return for helping them defeat the Christian City of Zara, a city on the Adriatic Sea. It was a shipping competitor of the Venetians. In November 1202, the crusaders and Venetians captured the City of Zara, killing many Christians.

This scheme worked well and the crusaders found the capture to be very profitable so it was easy for the Venetians to persuade the crusaders to wipe out another competitor, which was the great city of the Eastern Church, Constantinople. According to the account in <u>The Crusades</u> by Malcolm Billings, the Pope forgave them for killing Christians at Zara, because they were forced into it, but they were directed to return all stolen property and vow never to invade Christian lands again. A few of the crusaders took this to heart and went home but most ignored the Pope and agreed to a deal to restore the recently dethroned Isaac Angelus as Emperor of Constantinople. The Venetians and Angelus both saw an opportunity in hiring the crusaders. The Doge of Venetians could get a better trade agreement when Angelus would replace his brother Alexus III on the throne. The deal as reported, included Angelus paying two thousand silver marks plus an army of ten thousand Greeks to fight in the East for one year, plus a garrison of five hundred knights to stay in the Holy Land.

The Pope's communication forbidding the whole arrangement did not arrive in time. The Venetian ships with tall towers built on their decks were moved into position. The ship towers were higher than the fortification towers, so the crusaders gained the advantage. The knights broke through and the city fell in one day. This was a city that had warded off many, many attacks in the past. In July 1203 the crusaders were given three days to sack, pillage and rape throughout the beautiful city. Great wealth was found in the church coffers, which was divided as spoils of war. They divided up the land to establish the Latin period of control over the Eastern Church and territory. This drove the Orthodox Church into a small area now called Albania.

The next crusade, time wise, and the most regrettable, was the children's crusade. It seems that a Christian boy named Steven, twelve years old, had a dream or revelation in which God had told him that only young innocent children could drive the infidels out of the Holy City. His claim was that God gave him instructions to inform the king of his revelation, who promptly refused to permit any such poorly conceived idea.

Steven was not to be dissuaded and started to preach crusading to many children in the countryside. He was very enthusiastic, which rubbed off on other twelve year old boys and some girls. About thirty thousand marched with Steven, living off the land. After losing many to starvation, the balance reached the sea where the Venetians provided old ships to the children. Two ships sank with all hands lost at sea, while the balance of the boats made it across the Mediterranean, and the remaining children were sold into slavery.

During this period another child leader named Nicholas, raised an army who were a little older. Thousands followed him to convert the infidels to Christianity. During the march over the Alps to Rome many were killed or starved on the way. On their arrival in Rome the Pope refused to sanction the young people's attempt to free the Holy Land, and ordered them to go home. They were too tired for a trip back across the punishing Alps, so they dispersed into the villages and never returned home.

The fifth and sixth crusades did not accomplish their goal militarily, but Frederick, Emperor of Germany, negotiated with a weakened Muslim defense and again received visiting rights for the pilgrims to the Holy Land.

This didn't last long because the Turks captured the Holy Land. This caused the formation of the 7th crusade in 1249, led by Louis IX, who was captured and sold back for ransom. He then joined Edward of England to form the 8th and last Holy Crusade. Louis died of the plague and the crusade made an unfortunate end.

Crusades continued after the first infamous eight (1096–1270). The Pope saw an opportunity to utilize armies in places like Lithuania, Spain and Italy, for religious reasons in the same manner as the Holy crusades, by issuing indulgences. As in Constantinople and the slaughter of Arabs in Jerusalem, the crusades were at times extremely cruel. At one point the Pope sent a full crusade against political enemies, or gave

French men a license to fight other French men. The area was the south of France where a group called Cathars had formed in what the Pope had condemned as heresy. The area or civil control was under the Count of Taulouse, who would not suppress Catharianism. (They had a dual God of matter and spirit). In this case the Pope offered the crusaders a special forty-day indulgence for enlisting in the crusade. The reason for bringing this up, what would be strictly history, and not part of this book, is the storming of the City of Beziers. It resulted in Jews, Cathers and Catholic citizens fighting alongside each other to defend their city. The church where many sought shelter and the surrounding area, was burned with seven thousand people slaughtered. Malcolm Billings in <u>The Crusades</u>, reports that at the height of the battle, the knights were told that they were killing Christians as well as heretics. The Papal Legate said, "kill them all, God will know his own."

Of the knights that had been formed during the crusades, the Templars, although very rich at one point, were stripped of most of their assets. Many of the knights combined with the Hospitallers. The Teutonic knights also fell from grace and were accused of heresy and brutal practices. It was very difficult to disprove heresy and conviction served as a political weapon.

The longest lasting Knight organization was the Hospitallers, who were smart enough to capture the Island of Rhodes, where they could harbor their galleys. They built huge towers to protect the Island and lived a communal life. They worked in their hospitals, maintained their city, and fought on their galleys. They maintained life on Rhodes for over two hundred years.

The crusades, for over two hundred years, were more than a pursuit to free the Holy Land. They called it "Liberation Theology." They fought to cleanse their sins and to worship God. They sold their lands to raise money to go into battle. The Pope, through indulgences, promised to forgive them all their sins. It must be noted, however, that they had, to a great extent, influenced the history of Europe. This developed into an acknowledgment that an eastern expansion was blocked, so they must turn west. Not the least of the blockage was the Ottoman Empire. They fought and won all of the Byzantine Empire in the fourteenth century and by 1453 captured Constantinople. At one point they ruled over all of Asia Minor, the Balkan Peninsula, parts of Hungary and Russia, Syria, the Caucasus, Palestine, Egypt, Arabia, and North Africa. Even though Europe was looking for expansion, there was no way that they could expand East, and in a matter of a short time expansion would be West to the New World. The crusaders discovered new and exciting potential in their travels and found beautiful cities with much opulence and different cultures. Many of their stories, which they told on their return, those that were lucky enough to return, were exaggerated, which drove the desire for new frontiers.

During this period, the notorious, cruel and politically motivated Tribunal was created, which was called the Inquisition. Judges traveled the countryside, trying people for heresy. Devious means, including torture, were used to extract a confession. The victims could be fined, imprisoned for life, or burned at the stake. The system was very successful in disposing of political enemies or for revenge. According to Compton, inquisition reached its heights in Spain in 1480, where King Ferdinand and Queen Elizabeth used it to it's fullest and took control over the process which lasted until 1800.

The Middle Ages, 500–1500, came to a close with the fall of Constantinople in 1453, (which ended the Byzantine Empire), discovery of America in 1492, and the reformation in 1517. No one can even estimate how many people died in the crusades. In addition, those that lived were reduced to slaves, crippled, and most unable to return home. The Jews were subjected to a holocaust, all under the battle cry "God Wills It," and financed by indulgences for their sins.

Chronology of Chapter VI

1054	Schism between Roman and Orthodox churches.
1140	Buddhism reaches it's height in Korea.
1059	College of Cardinals is established to elect the Pope.
1095	First crusade to free the Holy Land.
1122	Diet of Worms confirms authority of the church over the Empire.
1130	Chu-Hsi revives Confucianism into comprehensive system of thought.
1204	Sack of Constantinople by the 4th crusade.
1209	Italian Francis of Assisi founds Franciscan order of Mendicant Monks.
1216	Spanish Theologian Dominic establishes Dominican Order.
1250	Italian Thomas Quinas writes on scholastic Theology.
1233	Inquisition created by Pope Gregory IX to abolish Heresy.
1409	There were three rival Popes at the same time.
1417	The election of Pope Martin V who finally deposed all rival Popes.
1450	First papal indulgences for the dead.

7

1500–1600 CE

❖

Reformation

As a prelude to the reformation, Desiderius Erasmus, an Augustinian, left the order and became a prolific writer. He wrote about the early Christians, wrote a Greek translation of the Bible, and suggested reforms of the Roman Church. He also wrote extensively about bringing the Church back to its roots in the New Testament. His cause was basically the same as later reformers, but he definitely did not support a reformation that would break up the Roman Church or divide it. His best known book was The Praise of Folly in 1509.

Most historians call John Wycliffe of England the morning star of the reformation. In 1374, after teaching at the Oxford University, he became rector of Lutterworth in Leicestershire. He objected strongly to the Pope's authority to tax and appoint men to church offices without the king's permission and was originally supported by the nobles but lost their support when he proclaimed that the nobles position and wealth was held only by God's grace. His teachings brought on a peasant revolt. His most notable work was directing the translation of the Latin Vulgate Bible into English. He argued that an individual could best make religious decisions based on the bible, and questioned not only the wealth of the Roman Church but also its teachings and the authority of the Pope and the Monastic Orders.

Wycliff's ideas were carried on in Prague by the Czech reformer Jan Hus, 1369–1415. He protested against the church with much of Wycliff's writing and ideas, but didn't agree with Wycliffe on transubstantiation and when he objected to the burning of Wycliff's books he was falsely accused of heresy. He is remembered most for translating the bible to Bohemian for the common people, which Compton explains, established Bohemian as a literal language. To say that the Pope was annoyed at him for burning the Pope's decree of indulgences to join a crusade, would be understating the case. Jan Hus was finally put to death in 1415.

The great western schism (not to be confused with the great Rome/Constantinople Schism) ran from 1378 to 1477. It all started when a French pope was selected and simultaneously there were threats to the sovereignty of the papal states (more or less central Italy). The papacy was moved to Avignon in southern France in 1305 where it remained until 1378. After seventy-five years the Papacy was returned to Rome at which time Pope Urban VI was elected in 1378. This was short lived after he was proven to have a mental illness. Realizing their error, another Pope was selected (Clement VII). Each Pope, however, then proceeded to excommunicate the other. Finally a church council was assembled in Pisa to settle many church issues and selected Alexander V to replace the two existing Popes. Unfortunately, however, the two didn't resign and a Cardinal said that a "Simultaneous Holy Trinity" ruled the church. The Great Western Schism ended with the Council of Constance in 1414–18 with the selection of Pope Martin V.

The Church in Rome had suffered a serious loss of power and prestige. The western church was suffering from a bad case of finances, patronage and dispensations, all being linked to an increased literacy among the laymen and the Renaissance. Powerful forces were in the wind with Wycliff in England and Jan Huss in Bohemia, translating the bible. This period, 1378 to 1477, the church calls a schism within the church.

William Tyndale, 1492–1536, working with the Wycliffe translation, but most importantly working with the best of the old Hebrew and Greek manuscripts available, published his English New Testament in Cologne because he was forced to flee England. He was later declared a heretic and burned at the stake.

Miles Cloverdale, 1488–1569, along with Knox, Wittingham, and Calvin working in Geneva, continued the work and produced the Geneva Bible. This was the first version to be divided into verses. Richard Tavernew produced the first English version to be published in England.

The Douai Bible was the Roman Catholic version or translation, written by two former Oxford men, William Allen and George Martin. The New Testament was issued in 1582 and the Old Testament by 1609, which became the accepted Bible of English speaking Roman Catholics.

The above points out that the general unfounded concept claimed that Luther wrote the only Protestant translation of the Bible, while in reality he was only a spoke in the wheel of progress from the list of the main early translators.

Shall we say that the plot thickens when Martin Luther took up the gauntlet in 1517. He had given up the study of law and entered the Augustinian Monastery. Most historians credited him with being an outstanding theologian and bible scholar. He earned his doctorate in 1512 and became professor of literature at the Wittenberg University. Luther became convinced of a theological disagreement with Rome in the area of faith, but the spark that lit the reformation fire began when the Pope sent a Monk, Johann Tetzel, to Germany to sell indulgences. Money was needed to build the cathedral in Rome. Luther felt the Pope was deceiving the people, in that you cannot buy forgiveness with money, and Luther came out fighting. He rejected the authority of the Pope and proclaimed the Bible as the Christian authority. He announced that the monks, nuns and monasteries were held under non-binding oaths, and should be done away with. He also objected to celibacy. Of the seven sacraments Luther only retained Baptism and the Eucharist. His main points were that you could not put a financial price on remission of sins (indulgences), that a person is saved by grace alone and the authority of the Pope is not based on the bible

After Luther wrote his 95 Thesis, explaining his position, he nailed them on the church door in Wittenberg. Imagine the audacity or conviction of Luther taking on the entire Holy Roman Empire (which actually was not Roman, holy, or an empire), in what he thought would be a debate to reform the church. The Pope promptly issued a Papal Bull (an order from the Pope), for Luther to recant. Spreading the thesis all over Germany fanned the flames of reform. A point could be made that Pandora's Box was opened.

The Bull of Excommunication against Luther was given to Emperor Charles V, who called the Council of Worms to examine Luther's activity and his contentions. Still demanding reform, he refused to recant and was declared an outlaw. He went into hiding, which afforded him the time to translate the Bible into German so the people could read and decide on the issues for themselves. Smoldering embers of discontent among the peasants were ignited by much of Luther's Thesis and a revolt ensued. At this point Luther failed the people because he supported the Princes to put down the revolt of the peasants.

Why was Luther's movement more widespread and successful than Hus or Wycliffe? Luther was furnishing much more documentation in a more convincing manner, which could be printed for circulation. The main catalyst was the invention of the Gutenberg printing press, which made massive circulation possible. Not the least of the catalyst was that the peasants were ready to revolt against their meager existence.

Just a word about the Gutenberg Press, which actually revolutionized the literary world. The first major attempt was a two column, forty-two line bible, which was referred to as the Mainzger Bible, because the first copy printed in Latin went to Cardinal Mainzger (who became Pope Justice II). The tremendous achievement of the press over hand written copies was not only the speed to produce manuscripts, but also duplication with accuracy.

Luther was often accused by the Catholic Church of starting the reformation so that he could marry a Nun. Historically, I find that is unlikely in that he started his battle against celibacy of priests in 1514, and didn't marry until 1525. I doubt if he intended to make a statement against celibacy that he would have waited ten years after starting the debate and five years after he was excommunicated to marry.

My socialistic professor of European History spent a whole lecture condemning Luther for deserting the peasants, leaving their support to Calvin and Zwingli. Another of his points was that by translating the bible to German, many more peasants learned to read, so that they could see for themselves what the Bible said. Prior to this time, reading was basically limited to nobles and the clergy, and when the peasants read, they learned more about the bible. This led to reading other works, such as socialistic philosophy. As a result of the work of Eramus, Hus, Wycliffe and Luther, the illiteracy rate dropped and it was but a relatively few years before constitutional government revolutions were started.

Calvin and Zwingli were more radical than Luther. Zwingli (1484–1531), was educated at the University of Vienna, and became a priest in 1506. It was not long before Zwingli argued that the people should interpret the bible for themselves. In 1518 he was made priest at the Grossmunster Cathedral in Zurich where he studied the work of Eramus. He started gradual changes in the church, and this caused public debate, but other churches followed his lead. He finally broke with Rome and agreed with Luther on the supremacy of the bible, but differed on the nature of the Eucharist. He also supported the peasant revolt, which caused a problem for Luther, and they each went their separate ways. Zwingli also denounced icons fanatically but it was the Anabaptists, a more radical group, who claimed Luther and Zwingli were only half reformist and they failed to define the goals of the reformation. The Anabaptists were outlawed, fined and imprisoned, but they were never silenced.

John Calvin (1509–1564) was considered by historians second only to Luther in importance to the reformation. His father was Secretary of the Diocese in Noyon, France. Calvin studied for the priesthood but at the age of twenty-two experienced a conversion to what he considered a simpler form of Christianity. He had to flee from France to Geneva, Switzerland, because of his outspoken objections to the Church of France. He attained great respect and a large following in Geneva. He was a prolific writer and conceived what was considered ideals of simplicity, purity, and a devout religious faith. Calvin is the forerunner or basis of the Presbyterian and Reformed Churches. These were the Huguenots of France, the Protestants of the Netherlands and Scotland, and the Puritans of England.

We have now reached a period of religious wars, which did not stop until the end of the thirty-year war in 1648. In 1555, the Peace of Augsburg, a religious agreement made by civil authorities, forced Charles V to grant each German State the right to choose between a Catholic and Lutheran State church. The peace was only temporary and families would be split, with brother fighting brother in war, all believing that their God was directing them.

In addition to Martin Luther and all the other reformers in the sixteenth century, the scientific theory of astronomy was giving the Roman Church a bit of a headache. The Church had, since day one, established a dogma that stated that the earth is the center of the universe, which was accepted by the Church. Claudius Ptolemaeus, around 100 CE, was working with Greek astronomy knowledge and produced evidence of the sun and stars revolving around the earth. The Bible propagated this theory. It is interesting to note that he also produced a calendar, a treatise on music, and produced a guide to geography, by using latitudes and longitudes. This was 1400 years before Copernicus who in 1530, by studying the stars, published his most important book on the heavenly bodies. Nicholas Copernicus, 1472 to

1543, was the founder of modern astrology, contradicting the Ptolemaic theory (which was the geocentric or earth centered theory). The Church called him a heretic and stopped the publication of his book for thirteen years. The great scientific achievement of the Polish astronomer would lead the way for Galileo and Johannes Kepler. Unfortunately, Copernicus died a persecuted and ridiculed scientist. The Christian Church, both Roman and Eastern, was trying to stop the theories of Copernicus during the same time that Martin Luther was questioning their misuse of the Bible.

On the scientific side, it would only be a few years before Galileo, 1564 to 1642, the father of modern physics, would substantiate the work of Copernicus by the use of a telescope. Although he never used his full name, it was Galileo Galilei. He worked in the field of mathematical theories, the pendulum which provides an accurate timepiece, and in the field of hydrostatics.

During the same period, Johannes Kepler published his laws of planetary motion in 1609, basing his work on Copernicus's theories. Galileo supported the work of Kepler and of course, Copernicus, so the church ordered him to cease and desist, which he would not do. He was put under house arrest for eight years until he died. It would be nearly four hundred years before Pope John Paul II, on behalf of the Roman Church, finally accepted his teachings. These pioneers in science were followed by Rene' Descartes, 1596 to 1650, where modern philosophy and mathematics began, especially geometry. He was determined to produce a first principal, which the Church could not dispute. Sir Isaac Newton, 1642 to 1727, is said to have been the chief figure in the scientific revolution due to his work with light, color, and the law of gravitation. The Church was, of course, still not accepting the respective position of the earth in the solar system. This was called the Scientific Revolution, which developed in the seventeenth and eighteenth century and was followed by the Renaissance. Another movement, the Age of Enlightenment, changed the traditional church. This was the age, which questioned man's destiny or the reason for his being. It is what Thomas Paine called the Age of Reason, as contrasted to the Christian attempt to explain all things by faith. This was serious business because the Church had been proven vulnerable to science.

The Age of Reason did not accomplish the distraction of faith, because faith had on its side a new revolt called Romanticism. It was mostly in the arts but dispelled the concept of science as the origin of natural reason, or the total answer to life. Reason could never totally replace faith because faith has an emotional uncompromising knowledge that there is a power stronger than reason, where in some situations faith may be the only answer. If you believe strong enough even the human body may react. This is a fact that faith healers use, even if in some cases it is merely temporary or imagined. This can be carried to the extreme by letting sick children die rather than seeking medical help because of the parent's faith that God will heal. This is not faith, it is a condition of mental instability brought on by overreacting to the saving grace in the Christian tradition of Christ. It is true, healing has existed as long as Christianity, but healing when all else fails, and faith becomes the only answer. It would be a far greater sin to pass up proper medical attention, knowing full well God's will may lie in the hands of the doctor or surgeon.

The question can be asked, did the Age of Reason do good or evil? The answer is both. They may have failed to replace faith and tradition, but they did introduce or develop, in the minds of the masses, new ideas in politics, law and economics, thus changing the course of history.

Before moving into the spread of religious philosophy, some important aspects or insurmountable differences coming out of the reformation should be cleared up. The main characters of the reformation demanding changes came from within the Roman Church, not from an outside force attacking it. They were Priests and highly educated leaders of religious orders, and theoretically took their revolutionary ideas from the Bible. At the Council of Trent the Roman Catholic Church admitted their mistakes and tried to correct them. It was too late, the common people were reading the Bible themselves. This was not a hasty event, because it ran its course from 1350 to 1648. The horrors of the killings were beyond comprehension. I once heard a professor lecturing on the reformation explaining that the blood ran ankle deep in the gutters of Germany, while brother was killing brother. Luther himself tried to persuade the German states to stop the peasants uprising but Zwingli and Calvin were not so inclined. Zwingli followers in particular, were so strongly obsessed with the idol worship of icons, that they not only entered the churches and destroyed all of the beautiful art in the alters, but killed anyone trying to stop them.

Jesus, like Buddha and Mohammed, never left a written word. Up until Paul convinced Rome to admit Luke, a gentile, into the Christian church, all the Christians had been Jewish Christians, with Jewish church traditions. It was a half-century after Jesus died, that the church was finally established, with it's own traditions, and the early Christians were starting to subject the faith to writing. The New Testament, however, was not agreed to until the year 200. It would be another one hundred years before Constantine decreed that there was a Christian Church and more years before they finally agreed on the Nicene Creed, which defined what the Christian Church believed. You could, therefore, pick the year 200 for the start of the Christian or Catholic Church, because it was no longer Jewish tradition, and they had a Testament to define their belief. As far as the Eastern Orthodox church claim to being the original Christian Church, it appears historically, that they were not a separate entity until Rome added the Filioque to the Nicene Creed, and they overrode the church rules against icons in 800. Their liturgies were not established until about the same time of St. John Chrysostom and St. Basil the Great. Unfortunately, the two greatest issues driving the reformation were indulgences, Doctrine of Justification (Roman) and icons (Orthodox), which was considered by Protestants as idol worship.

Could the reformation have been stopped, or put another way, could we all agree and become one happy Church family? Several stumbling blocks will prevent this. The Protestants may never accept the hallowed position of Mary in the Catholic Church, never accept celibacy, and never accept confessions to priests, never accept icons, and probably never accept the authority of the Pope. Pandora's box is open, and what a mess we have made out of the teachings of Jesus to twelve ordinary citizens on a little dot of the world map. We have taken a relatively few words from Jesus and interpreted them in a thousand ways.

One of the important results of the reformation is the translation of the Holy Bible. There are three distinct books, the Jewish, Protestant and the Catholic. The Bible is a collection of books and as we have explained in Chapter II, of unknown authors. The oldest is the Jewish, which consists of twenty-four books called Canon (authoritative). The Jewish Bible is divided into three major groupings. The law is the oldest, which includes the first five books. This was recognized as Jewish Canon in the sixth century BCE. The second group is the Prophets, which is not to prophesy the future or foretell the future, but to translate the law and condemn the breaking of the law. This part was made Canon in the third or fourth century BCE. The third group is the writings, which is a collection of stories, poetry and history. These are very important to both Christian and Jewish education, the best known being the Psalms.

At this point the Apocrypha (not canonical, of dubious authority), is separated from the Canon in both the Jewish and the Protestant Old Testaments. The Catholic Old Testament gathered nearly all of the books. The Jewish Bible has twenty-four books, while the Protestant Old Testament, due to rearranging and numbering, came up to thirty-nine books, but basically they were the same. The Old Testament Laws and Prophets were well established by the second and third century BCE, but Jewish Rabbis established the final selection of the writings as Canon in Palestine, about 100 CE, which completed the Jewish Bible.

The Christian Bible includes the Old Testament, but adds the New Testament. Here the division of religious theology between Jews and Christians is split forever. It is a matter of understanding that the Old Testament is a covenant that the Jewish fathers believe was made between the Jews and God. They were to be the chosen people. The Christian view is that Jesus the Christ, a Jew, changed that because they had not lived up to their law. One might get this impression when you consider the Jews were conquered by Rome, Babylon, Persia, Assyria, and scattered throughout the world, subject to repeated holocausts.

The New Testament is divided into the Gospels, Act of the Apostles, the Epistles, and Revelations. The Gospels are called the good news, which describe the life of Christ, but are also a statement of faith about him. The Acts are missionary reports. The Epistles, which are the most numerous, are letters of which twenty-one out of twenty-seven are written by St. Paul. These letters were written earlier than the Gospels, and were copied and distributed wherever a Christian Church was formed. The most difficult book to interpret and understand is Revelations. It is said to be colorful and imaginative and stresses that the Kingdom of God is near. It is interesting to note, at this point, that many of the early Christians believed the second coming of Christ was imminent and in their lifetime.

The Jewish and Protestant Bibles of the Old Testament are basically the same, but the Catholics added books, which were not accepted by the Jewish fathers as Canon, although they were popular at one time, and read by Jews. They did not compliment or add to the twenty-four books established as Canon. The books in question are, I and II Esdras, Tobit, Judith, additions to the book of Esther, Wisdom of Solomon, Ecclesiastics, Baruch, Song of the Three, Daniel and Susanna, Bell and the Dragon, and First and Second Maccabees. The Catholic Church recognizes all but First and Second Esdras as authoritative.

Before ending a discussion of the Jewish Old Testament and parts of the New Testament it should be noted that when St. Augustine referred to the Bible he explained "some of the practices and teachings of the apostles no longer apply to Christians because the apostles lived in a different age." Albert Schweitzer said that the authors of the bible wrote with the knowledge they possessed at that time. The authors of the Old Testament were writing or converting oral tradition a millennium after the fact. They wrote based on their knowledge of science and their environment. The earth is not flat, however, and the sun does not orbit around the earth. It was 1600 CE before the Catholic Church accepted this fact. The authors of Geneses (J) most likely received the idea of the seven-day concept of creating the earth from the Sumarians who counted the week in this way, two to three hundred years prior. The Sumarians had established that people would work six days and the seventh would be for recreation. It must be acknowledged that infinite details in the bible may not be accurate today. Archeologists have proven many of the stories revealed in the bible are true, many are not, and many are partially true. A priest who had been questioned about a fact in the bible, stated that religion is not a science but rather a faith and we will leave it at that.

We have mentioned in previous chapters other works that have served an important role. The earliest was the Septuagint written supposedly by seventy-two scholars of the Tribe of Judea, around the third century BCE. It was the Bible used by early Christians before there was a New Testament, which was translated from Hebrew to Greek. In 400 CE St. Jerome wrote a Latin translation of the Hebrew Bible, called the Latin Vulgate, which included some Apocryphal books which the Roman and Greek Church accepted as Canon, even though they were not accepted by Hebrew tradition and were not in the Septuagint, although they were written by Jews. The Vulgate remained the chief bible until the reformation.

James I, King of England, 1603–25, (one hundred years after Henry VIII, split with the Pope) and made an important contribution to the Protestant translation of the Bible with a more scientific process. King James selected fifty-four scholars to start with all the Bible translations available, which would include Erasmus, Luther, Tyndale, Cloverdale, the Geneva Bible, the Douai Bible, plus the entire original Arabic and Hebrew work. He utilized theologians and linguists in Hebrew, Arabic, Latin and Greek, to translate and write the King James Version. It has served as the authentic Protestant Bible for 250 years until the golden age of biblical translations in the 19th and 20th centuries. By 1870 many valuable manuscripts of the Bible had been found and accumulated so a committee from England and the United States were appointed to produce a bible with modern translation information and reduce the errors, which had resulted from the old English words. This was called the revised King James edition. The American committee felt that the English were too conservative and in 1901 produced the Bible known as the American Standard Revised Edition.

The Dead Sea Scrolls found in 1947, contained parts of all of the Old Testament writings. They also include some heretofore-unknown books. The Naghammadi finds in 1945 contain material from the School of Gnosticism that had been buried in 200 CE. Most of it did not represent teachings of the New Testaments but clarified some of the debates of the early Christians.

Chronology of Chapter VII

1506	St. Peters Basilica started in Rome.
1517	Martin Luther begins the Protestant Reformation.
1518	Zwingli starts Swiss Reformation.
1520	Luther is excommunicated as heretic.
1520	Anabaptist starts in Switzerland.
1530	Augsburg confession defines Lutheran beliefs.
1534	Society of Jesus (Jesuits) is formed.
1534	English Reformation begins.
1536	Calvin starts Reformation in Geneva which spreads to France (Huguenots).
1545–1563	Council of Trent establishes Roman Catholic reforms.
1549	England adopts Book of Common Prayer.
1552	Archbishop of Canterbury publishes Articles of Anglican faith.
1553	Queen Mary of England reestablishes Catholic religion.
1555	Peace of Augsburg, State can now determine it's own religion.
1555	First Reformed Church is formed in France.
1558	Queen Elizabeth reestablishes Protestant religion in England.
1560	Pope Pius V excommunicates Elizabeth.
1560	Scotland establishes Presbyterian Doctrine.
1572	Massacre of St. Bartholomew's Day.
1590	Russia becomes independent Patriarchal.

8

1600–To Date

❖

Getting Organized

The Reformation brought on not only human conflict and wars, but also a scurry of activity in creating new philosophical religious concepts for each of many groups. It starts with Luther, who realized that the 95 Thesis nailed to the door of the church would need proof and theological direction. Luther's main solution was translating the bible into German, and not the least was his catechism so that he could relate the details of the Lutheran Church briefly and they would become an instructional tool for children and confirmands. Luther, Wycliffe and Hus all agreed on one point, that the bible was the sole authority and source of Christian faith. The Lutheran Church spread in Northern Germany and Scandinavia and is much the same today.

In addition to all the denominations that were forming on every front, Lutheranism had diverse ideas within its ranks. The most persuasive was Pietism, which is defined by Webster as emphasis on devotional experiences and practices, which stress bible study and good works. This was a reaction to the strict dogmatism. In these thoughts you can detect the extreme opposite to Orthodox Catholic doctrine. If the split in theological differences were not visible before, it certainly would be now. This, of course, was manifested in all the radical departures from Lutheranism and Anglianism.

Another group affected by Pietism were the Moravian Brethren in Bohemia whose origin was from the fifteenth century Hussites of

Bohemia and Moravia. In addition to being a Christ centered non-violent group, they stressed hymns and worship and published the first Protestant hymnbook. This is the group that had such a positive effect on John Wesley in England, who we will discuss later. The Moravians finally arrived in America in 1734, at which time they sent missionaries to the Indians and the underprivileged. They also sent missionaries to South America, Africa, and Greenland, among others.

The Roman Catholic Church called the Council of Trent, 1545 to 1563, to issue decrees to correct abuses and reaffirm ancient doctrines which they had obviously been getting away from. Compton makes a good point, in that the next few Popes were good administrators, enabling them to take back at least part of the territory they lost in the Reformation. In general the Council of Trent was too little and too late.

The French Protestants were called Huguenots, although no one knows where the name came from. Many French nobles became Protestants, which is evident in eight separate wars or battles in the middle sixteenth century. One of the main characters was Gaspard de Coligny, with the title of Admiral who was head of the Protestant cause in France. After the other leaders were killed, he took command and demanded religious freedom. Although he had gained the respect of King Charles IX, Catherine de Medici, the Queen Mother, plotted against Coligny and had him assassinated. She then planned and carried out a general massacre of Protestants, cleverly setting the time when most of the leading Huguenots were in Paris at the wedding of King Navarre (later King Henry IV of France).

On the night of 24 August 1572, at the Feast of St. Bartholomew, the order was given for the general massacre of French Protestants called Huguenots. Estimates of the dead were at least twenty thousand killed (three thousand in Paris alone). This was called the Massacre of St. Bartholomew's Day.

Coligny had sent three unsuccessful Huguenot Colonies to the New World. They had actually been forbidden to leave France, but they did, taking with them French art and culture to England, Germany, the Netherlands and the British Colonies.

Presbyterianism was created from the reformed church organized in Switzerland and Southern Germany by Zwingli and John Calvin. The name comes from self-governing or Presbyters, meaning Elders. Elders, who were to be elected by the congregation, governed the early churches.

The Reformation started in England when Henry VIII broke with the Catholic Church in 1534. It is generally believed that the break came when the Pope refused to sanction Henry's marriage. This is true, but there was another more pressing issue, which may have been Henry's main objective. The Church was very wealthy, with a full treasury, which Henry needed badly to prepare for a war with France, and to build England's first Navy. The Cardinal refused the loan but it was a simple matter to just take over the Church coffers, because there was already a rising tide of reformation in the country. Henry wanted to keep the Church exactly as it was, except without the Pope. Reform was in the air, however, and under Edward VI, Protestantism was successful in England. One more stumbling block came up under the period of Mary Tudor, a Roman Catholic who re-established the Roman Catholic Church. When Elizabeth I took the throne, Protestantism became permanent.

The Reformers as they were called, were divided in four doctrinal differences. The first was the Episcopal (Bishop control). This developed into the Church of England (Anglican). The next group, the Presbyterian Church, wanted to do away with the Bishop but would retain the State Church. The third group, Congregationalist, followed more closely to Knox, Calvin, and the Swiss reformers and they would reject all customs and traditions of the Roman Church, which were not proven as acceptable in the New Testament. They stripped all ornate vestments, religious images and pictures from the alters. The fourth was a radical faction, called Separatists, or Independents, who insisted on the separation of Church and State. Each congregation was to manage its own Church. Congregationalists were positioned between the Presbyterians and the Radicals (Baptists and Quakers).

During the reign of Charles I and the rebellious period in England, the Westminster Assembly, 1643–52, drew up a form of Church government, and a directory for public worship, This became standard for Presbyterians in England, Scotland and North America.

After the rebellion, Oliver Cromwell governed England with the power of the army. The religious pressure was for anti-Presbyterianism, which then resulted in an Episcopal form of Church government.

We should add a note of concern on the part of the Church of England (Anglican), in that they did not acknowledge that Henry VIII created the Church, regardless of his motives. They claim the Church existed for centuries in England, and grew from the earliest Church. The Office of Bishops dates its origin from the time of Jesus' Apostles. They, like the Greek Orthodox, claim "from the original." The Church Head, or spiritual leader, is the Archbishop of Canterbury. This title started in a very old city in England, which was there when Julius Caesar invaded England in 55 BCE. In 43 CE, Roman Emperor Claudius established an important base at this location and in 200 CE it became a walled city, which partially exists today. St. Augustine converted a ruler named Ethelbert, King of Kent, to Christianity, and Canterbury became the center of Christianity in England, which it still is today. St. Augustine ordered a cathedral built and as a reward, Pope Gregory I made him Archbishop of Canterbury. The title remains as the authority in the Church of England, the center of Anglican Communion.

The established Episcopal Church of England tried to stay as close as possible to the Roman Church, except they established the Bible as the authority for Christian belief. They maintain the ancient creeds of the Apostles Creed, the Nicene Creed, plus the four doctrines of the Councils of Nicaea, Ephesus, Constantinople and Chalcedon. They also added the Book of Common Prayer, which is revised from time to time and varies by areas. Their priests do not practice celibacy, and the

Immaculate Conception Dogma of Mary is not a part of any religion except the Roman Catholic. In 1689 the English Bill of Rights required the King to be a Protestant, which was followed in 1701 by the Act of Settlement, which required that the King be a member of the Church of England. As English explorers gained footholds in India, Africa, the Far East and America, their Missionary Armies set up Church groups, which would become the Anglican Communion. This is a very loose confederation with no over-riding authority to direct church activity except for Missionary work.

The Church of England, which is included in the Anglican Communion, is divided into dioceses, which are governed by a Bishop (there are four hundred diocese in the world). The larger group is called a Province, of which the USA has nine, and Japan one. The names of the many member churches vary, for example, Anglican Church of Australia, Episcopal Church of Brazil, Holy Catholic Church of China, Episcopal Church of Jerusalem, and the Protestant Episcopal Church in the USA.

At this juncture we can identify a basic group of churches maintaining the Roman Catholic style or traditional worship service. These are the Roman Catholics, Lutherans, and the Anglicans. As time progressed even the majority of the Lutherans drifted out of this category except the Missouri and Wisconsin Synods. Outside of this group, a new phenomenon took place in that the church attendees were not just audiences, but participants in worship and the decisions applying thereto. They rejected any form of symbolism as in icons, vestments, stained glass, incense and even music. Fortunately, music participation has been modified with time. It can be said that the changes reduced the austerity of the First Reformation Decrees. As we continue with the forming of what is called the diversification of Protestant churches, it will be obvious that a whole gamut of beliefs will be created over four hundred years of searching for the answer to God's will.

John Wesley was born in Lincolnshire, England, where his father was Rector of a church. After his education at Oxford, he became an assistant to his father. The story about the origin of Methodists begins when Wesley took a trip to America. He heard of and became interested in a group of reformers from Austria, called Moravians, which were related to Arminianism formed by the Dutch reformer Jacobus Arminius in 1609. Arminius concluded that God would elect for salvation those who had faith and accepted God's offer of salvation. On his return to England he attended group meetings of Moravians in London. He soon had a group join him as he discussed religion from a more austere approach. The group was called the Holy Club, which was due to their austere manners and methodical ways. Hence the name Methodist. He first started to preach in Churches, but they soon refused him their pulpit. He was not discouraged and simply started to preach in tents and in open areas, and was soon selecting ministers and organizing groups or churches. The movement spread, with thousands attending his churches. Wesley no doubt was the model for many charismatic itinerant preachers who started churches in America under tents, drive-in theaters or in rented theater buildings.

Of the more radical reformers, the Anabaptists were the left wing of the reformers, who would repudiate any form of Roman Catholicism in their attempt to seek the true apostolic church. They originated in the seventeenth century as an offshoot of the Congregationalists. The Ana was soon dropped. The Lutheran-Anglican-Episcopal movement, on the other hand, were the conservative or magisterial (taken from Britannia) reformers, who would at least try to keep whatever it could of the Ecclesiastical tradition of the Roman Catholic Church. There were two Baptist groups. The Particular Baptist and the General Baptist. Although it may be a bit confusing, the Particular Baptists believed that Christ died only for the elect (Calvin teaching). The General Baptists believed in a general atonement that Christ died for all people, not just the elect. The General Baptists came from the English Separatist Movement, while the Particular Baptists were non-Separatist. The General Baptists faded into the Quakers. The First Baptist Church was established in Amsterdam in 1608 and in London in 1611. The influence of the Puritans in England was felt when in 1643 England outlawed the celebration of Christmas, Easter and All Saint's Day. They consider these holidays a sacrilegious and hypocritical celebration. When the people refused to obey they outlawed mince pie and plum pudding that was a part of the holiday tradition. All was soon retracted and back to normal by 1660.

The Anabaptists spawned several faiths or beliefs that are so interrelated as to be indistinguishable to the layman trying to look at just the history of the whole picture. The Mennonites were first formed from the teaching of Menno Simons, a Dutch priest. At this point the Anabaptists would be considered moderate. The Mennonites were first called Swiss Brethren in 1525, who diligently fought the state church formed by Zwingli. One of the first battles in the schism that followed concerned the baptism of infants as contrasted to waiting until what they called an age of reason. The followers of Hans Hut in 1527 CE, and Pilgrim Marpeck, both theologians, formed another Anabaptist movement in 1556 and are credited with starting the Hutterian Brethren. The third group was the Amish, also called the Old Order Amish Mennonites. They were the followers of Jacob Ammann, a seventeenth century Mennonite elder, whose teachings caused another schism. His insistence of uniformed dress, untrimmed beards, but no mustache, caused a debate, which was finally agreed on. The Amish main goal was to maintain biblical dedication and discipline. All three groups spread across Holland, Germany and Switzerland.

The radical reformers grew in every country, even Catholic Italy (but not for long). They tried to throw out much of what Luther wanted to retain. Debates were mostly over baptism and the Lord's Supper in Switzerland, Southern Germany, Bohemia and the Netherlands. In Northern Germany and part of the Netherlands, the newly formed Mennonites carried the radical reformation into Poland and Eastern Germany.

The period of world exploration was under way. The Spanish and Portuguese sailed toward the south and did not have the desire, or it was not their main objective to colonize. They did set up Roman Catholic Missions as they progressed. The French on a much lesser scale explored the Saint Lawrence to the north. They were seeking furs not settlements. The English had sent John Cabot to explore the eastern coast of America.

After Queen Elizabeth (1558–1603), re-established Protestantism in England, she gave Sir Walter Raleigh a charter to explore and settle on the shore of the Carolinas in America. The first attempt resulted in conflicts with unfriendly Indians and a scarcity of supplies, which caused him to return the Puritans to England in 1587. He tried again soon after and set up a settlement on Roanoke Island, consisting of approximately one hundred people. John White, the Governor of the colony, returned to England for supplies, which took three years because of wars in Europe. When he returned he found a settlement not only deserted, but only one clue as to what had happened which was the word "Croatoan" carved in a tree. The best and only answer was that the Croatan Indians took them into captivity, intermarrying with the women and killing the men. The Croatan Indians, in later generations, did have some physical characteristics and some English names to make this answer plausible.

Jamestown, Virginia established the First Church in America and was the first permanent colony founded in 1607. The King had granted a charter to the Virginia Company of London to settle and explore part of the Virginia coast of the New World. Unfortunately they settled in low land, swampy and very unhealthy for those newcomers not accustomed to this environment. As a result many died. The settlement finally became successful when they started to grow tobacco for exporting. In 1619, the first legislative assembly in America was established and the first black slaves were imported from Africa.

The English did not have the money to continue developing the area. They did have a lot of religious zealots that they would have liked to get rid of and who wanted a place to practice their religion freely. The English came up with a scheme to kill two birds with one stone.

They issued charters to business groups anxious to gamble on big profits from the New World. Finding people anxious to go was no problem. The Puritans had been persecuted for so long that dying in the wilderness was not such a bad option because they would gain freedom of religion.

During the early reign of James I in 1608, a small group of Separatists were protesting that the King did not permit freedom of religion. They were called Puritans because they set out to purify the state Church, or they were called Separatists because they demanded a separate denomination. They were constantly persecuted and therefore fled to the Netherlands. It was not comfortable for them there, not being able to use their native language and traditions. They decided to contract with the Virginia Company, one of the companies that England had granted a charter to go to the New World where they could keep their native language and practice their faith.

As expected they didn't have the finances, so the merchants of the Virginia Company made an arrangement whereby the Pilgrims would share their output in America with the merchants for seven years. It was not a fair deal but they were anxious to get to the New World. They were assigned to the Mayflower, which was a one hundred foot, three-mast vessel. Historians still wonder how they all found a place to sleep. The Puritans numbered only half of the total passengers because the merchants sent people along to make sure that the Puritans lived up to their contract.

The trip took sixty-six days of incredibly bad conditions, landing near Plymouth. After a month of searching they decided on Plymouth for their settlement. They had missed Virginia, which was supposed to be their destination, and they would call the Plymouth area home. The ship remained for the winter because it was December 21 before they found the spot for their settlement in Plymouth. The last thing they did on the ship was to pray for deliverance and agree on a Church covenant adaptable for a civil government ashore. This was the first plan for self-government by European colonists in America. Unfortunately they chose a commune type community, not only for their idea of Utopia, but it would be easier to separate the merchant's share of their produce. I had made a note from a previous history class, which claims that religious groups had often tried to create a more perfect religious experience and existence by forming the perfect society or life in a Utopia, by following the basic structure of a commune. They have all failed.

The New England winter was well under way as they began to organize. Their small open boat moved through icy water, back and forth to the ship. They constructed buildings on shore from the plentiful trees for lumber and had good water from a fresh water stream. Unfortunately, the Pilgrims were not skilled at hunting or fishing, so the settlers were very fortunate that the native Indians were very friendly and taught them to hunt, plant corn and fish. They also taught them to catch herring to use as fertilizer for their crops. They still could not produce efficiently, because of the commune arrangement in which they gathered crops, furs and timber, to put in storage to be handed out as shares to the settlers, and part to be shipped to England to pay off their debt. Working in a commune situation, the men would be careful not to do more than their neighbor.

In 1627, after six years of near starvation, some land was finally granted to each man and they started to produce on their own farms. Wives and children would then help in the fields and the men worked longer and harder hours. By 1630–40, they were very productive and sold corn and livestock to the Massachusetts Bay Company settlers. This success brought about a reduction in Church dependency, and prayer was augmented with hard work. People moved on to find more acres or pastures. By 1691 the settlement was made part of Massachusetts and the New Congregational Church absorbed the Pilgrims. It is interesting to note that the term Pilgrim was not used until they were called Pilgrims in a speech by a Governor in 1820, two hundred years after the settlement.

The story of Thanksgiving dinner has many variations. It appears to be a fact that on one occasion a large band of Indians brought turkeys and several deer to the little group of settlers to celebrate the first harvest that had been gathered. The Indians were no doubt proud of the progress the Pilgrims had made with their help in maintaining life in a strange country. They had taught them the rules of existence, which would contribute to the reversing of the commune to the American spirit of free enterprise.

The Massachusetts Bay Colony, under Governor John Winthrop was given a Charter to settle with one thousand Puritans between the Charles and the Merrimack rivers. Normally the Charter Company would be required to hold yearly meetings in London to report on their progress, but it was left off the contract. The stockholders transferred control to America. They made it law that all members of the government must be members of the Puritan church.

The Separatists of Plymouth and the Puritanism of the Massachusetts Bay had an affinity sufficient to join in a declaration of faith, but maintained a Congregational Polity. Here we find an extension of the radical commitment of the spiritual intensity that could not maintain itself in the second generation. The high standard had to be relaxed. The community was greatly interested in education, however, which brought about the founding of Harvard College in 1636. This was only the first in the line of colleges under Congregational auspices in America.

The loss of religious fervor caused serious concern but new life and dedication came as the result of the Great Awakening, a widespread revival movement in 1720–40. At the same time rationalism had led religion to an emphasis on the human role in redemption, the emphasis on ethic plus de-emphasis on doctrine and tradition. It is important to know that revivalism did more than create schisms in the Protestant churches. It brought many non-churched into a church environment. In addition it contributed to the rise of woman's rights, abolition of slavery, and the women's right to vote. The direction to Congregationalism was a condition of the pendulum swinging from the Puritan unequivocal devotion to the bible, creeds and the public proclamation of one's God given blessings, to a Congregational control of the worship service, eliminating outward witnessing. Some might call it a simpler, more beautiful and less demanding service. This also brought about a growing Unitarianism which is a free use of reason and reducing the status of Jesus to a highly respected Prophet as do the Muslims.

The Amish started migrating to the United States around 1700. One large group of Mennonites came from Russia where they had been sought to stimulate agriculture in Russia. They were very successful and were rewarded with exemption from military draft. Later governments dropped the draft deferment so a large contingent immigrated to the United States. They also settled in smaller numbers in South America. In the United States they were located in Pennsylvania, Ohio, Indiana, Iowa, Illinois and Kansas. The Hutterites settled more toward the west and centered in South Dakota. It is impossible to differentiate in detail between the groups because of the constant shifting of attitudes and/or theology of the individual centers. When the old traditionalists refused to concur on modern issues, a new center was created.

There are certain practices common to the older groups, both Mennonite and Amish. They baptize when a grown young person joins the church, with the washing of feet in the worship service, they have a uniform dress code with buttons and hooks instead of zippers. They maintain small groups or centers so that they can live in contact with each other and attend church in their homes or barns. Most groups never have a church building. The horse drawn buggy or farm equipment is their main source of power, but in a few modern groups they have pickup trucks and tractors. Their language was a combination of English and German called Pennsylvania Dutch. They hold communion services twice a year.

All things change, however, and although they still teach their children in their private schools, they comply with state standards and educate their children until the legal age is met. Higher education is now possible because they are supporting their own colleges and seminaries. They are still pacifist and refuse military service, so if one of their own does join the service, he is in most cases excommunicated.

The Friends or Quakers were originally called Seekers. The majority came from the Puritan bodies, Presbyterians, Congregationalists or Baptists. They claimed powers directly from God but were severely persecuted for their firm beliefs. It appears the whole Puritan movement was attempting to stop the spread of Friends. At one time fifteen thousand were in prison, with five hundred dead in the process. They were still tenacious and sent members to America in 1656. Even the Quaker women preachers were active in Maryland, Massachusetts and Rhode Island. The most important Quaker Colony was in Pennsylvania, where William Penn, a Quaker convert, had secured a charter from the King of England, to set up what Penn called "A Holy Experiment." It was to test whether a state could exist with a firm position of pacifist and religious toleration, which would leave the state without military defense. Penn financed the project with the inheritance from his Father who had been an Admiral in the British Navy. High cost of the Colony and poor financial management forced him to file bankruptcy and serve a term in debtor's prison. The Quakers remained a force in Pennsylvania politics for many years. It can only be said regarding Pacifism that the Quakers treated the Indians better than most groups and had more friends among the Indians. The Colony was finally taken over by the crown of England. In America it should be noted that Quakers split over the support for the war. They were, however, determined to enforce a religious revival to help the poor, support education, improve prisons, and introduce temperance. Quakers made up a majority in most of the anti slavery groups.

William Penn's community is credited with the first establishment to recognize religious liberty or toleration and he welcomed all religions. The pioneer of religious liberty, however, was Roger Williams, 1604–83, a Seeker and adherent of Calvin theology. He purchased land from the Narragansett Indians and established the town of Providence in the Rhode Island Colony. He had been banished from the Massachusetts Bay Colony because of his radical views, which included the separation of Church and State. The theory of the separation of Church and State will continue and grow and was included in the United States Constitution.

The introduction of Christianity in North America to the southern area and the Gulf of Mexico was started with the settlement of St. Augustine in Florida and New Orleans in Louisiana. In 1565 the Spanish began an occupation of Florida with a stronghold in St. Augustine. Lines of Roman Catholic Missions with military outposts were located along the Georgia Coast. They were more successful at converting the Indians than in other areas. It was not until late in the seventeenth century that British pressure forced out the Spanish. French Huguenots, in 1564, established Fort Carolina near what is now Jacksonville, Florida. The Spaniards from St. Augustine massacred most of the French settlers in 1565, but Protestantism was not wiped out.

The first English settlement in Georgia was not established until 1633. Savannah was part of this movement. The area was started under charter, but was not productive enough to satisfy the trustees and the British government took over in 1672.

The Methodist movement had made their gains where the Church of England was weakest, namely in the countryside, small villages, crowded industrial areas, and the hill country. The Methodists also brought hymns into their service, following the Lutheran tradition as promoted by Martin Luther (himself an author of many hymns). Hymns would soon thereafter spread to the Church of England, the Congregationalists and the Baptists.

The "Holiness Movement" started with John Wesley in England, originator of the Methodist Church, who preached that an individual could achieve perfection in a lifetime. He concluded that if God could forgive sins, God could lead a believer into perfection. Within the Methodist Church not all believed this, although some felt it was the main doctrine of their church. Those falling in line with this belief formed the Free Methodist Church.

In France, in 1598, the Edict of Nantes, which gave religious freedom to the Huguenots, was also followed by exploration. The first was Arcadia, which would later be called Nova Scotia. This was followed by Samuel deChamplain in 1603, who explored the St. Lawrence, and founded Quebec in 1608. He defeated the Iroquois Indians, opening the route to fur hunting and sent trappers to The Great Lakes and finally to the Mississippi river and down to the Gulf of Mexico.

The Jesuit Order (Society of Jesus) was the principal missionary arm of the Roman Catholic Church. The Roman Church did not become a permanent establishment in this area as it did in the Spanish areas from Mexico to all of South America. This, of course, was due to the English settling all of Canada except the Quebec French area. Credit for spreading Christianity across Canada must be acknowledged as the life threatening, dangerous but dedicated work of the Jesuits. They gained routes in Canada even if their attempt to convert the Indians was in the end never successful. They became, in some cases, martyrs, as they followed the fur traders west through what is now Wisconsin, down the Mississippi to the Gulf of Mexico and out to the Dakotas. According to Britannica the fur trapping actually reduced the settling of permanent areas because the young, vigorous Frenchmen went off to seek their fortunes in furs instead of cultivating the land and establishing roots in one place. Religious leaders received neither tithes nor land dues from people in transit.

The Settlement of Louisiana was started by Spain but colonized by the French. New Orleans was established in 1718 by the French, which becomes important to this historical document because of the Arcadians. Above, we discussed the Arcadia Area (Nova Scotia), which after it became an English controlled area, the Arcadians refused to swear allegiance to the Crown, or the Church of England. This resulted in the Arcadians being exiled, with no place to go. Here we have ex-Huguenot Protestants (French), traveling down the British

East Coast who soon discovered that no one would give them an opportunity to relocate. As they progressed south, they found their new home in New Orleans, in an area inundated with swamps, alligators and snakes. The river area north of New Orleans was also the destination of thousands of Germans, and of course, the original French settlers. The area became a blend of Protestant and Catholic religions. Henry Wadsworth Longfellow portrays the Arcadians in the poem "Evangeline."

The Orthodox Church in America was formerly the "Russian Orthodox Greek Catholic Church of America" and was introduced in North America in 1794, in Alaska, which was Russian territory. With the sale of Alaska to the United States in 1867, the Episcopal seat of the Church was moved to San Francisco. In 1905 they transferred to New York City.

During this time period there was only a tiny American Jewish Community, which was the result of Sephardic (exiled) immigrants. The Jews were Orthodox but were experiencing changes due to the environment. As the early settlers moved west, the Jews also moved west as storekeepers and traders.

Religion in the 1700s was the catalyst for continued exploration, revivalists and free enterprise. The Great Awakening, 1720-40, is said to have spread like wildfire and provided a pulpit with great power. Was the Great Awakening a success, probably not, because it ran out of steam before 1740. At the end only one in ten citizens attended church, and churches were losing members in alarming rates. Success can be measured in many ways, however. At least one result was the springboard from which came the driving force for revolution. The Great Awakening was led by Jonathan Edwards, who was later condemned in his own church because of many unfavorable moves, not the least of which was going back to the early Puritan requirement of members having to stand to make short public confessions. The congregation finally transferred him to an isolated church in the outback where he spent his time writing.

George Whitefield, an Anglican minister from England, continued the revival with great success, but when he returned to England the flames were dimming.

In New England several individuals spoke out and are remembered for their contribution to the American Revolution. Best known, of course, were Sam Adams and John Hancock, but equally important were the two lawyers who fought in the Supreme Court on behalf of the merchants, namely James Otis and Oxenbridge Thatcher. The church was equally represented in this group by the Congregationalist Reverend Jonathan Mayhew, who was called "the morning gun of the revolution," and preached from the important pulpit of the West Church in New York City. He eventually denied the deity of Jesus Christ, rejected the doctrine of the Trinity, and became a Unitarian. He was a robust, brilliant preacher, but only the start of a long line of preachers who from the pulpit would guide and direct the people to revolution. Benjamin Franklin and Thomas Jefferson, both deists, never hesitated to utilize the church to gain support for the revolution. The early theories of Roger Williams on the separation of church and state became part of the United States Constitution.

John Adams, in his book <u>Yankee Doodle Went to Church</u> describes a little known and pertinent part of history called the Anglican Episcopal Controversy. It was based on the fear that England was sending Bishops to the Episcopal Churches in the colonies with the eventual results that the Bishops would have sufficient control in various areas. The British King could control the American territory without any kind of conflict. It is said that the Colonists had such fear of the Bishops that Paul Revere could just as well have said "The Bishops are Coming" to spread the same alarm, instead of "The British are Coming."

The sparks of the Great Awakening fanned the flame of revivalism through the nineteenth century by way of the western movement. Itinerant preachers, most of them lay preachers, moved west with the expanding frontier. It must be noted that in many cases religion was a closer tie to the old world than it was to the new secular society. The revivalists drew followers from the established churches because they did not have a presence in the west. New forms of services and individual conversion were more important than traditional organized churches. Many preached that the Second Coming of Christ was at hand, so you must get right with the Lord today or it will be too late. The countryside was dotted with little wood framed buildings, which held small groups of people for church services. Unfortunately most of the conversions were temporary because of their continual movement or just being too busy keeping alive, to attend church. These little churches were very important, however, because they did convert many to a Christian life and most importantly they helped to bring law and order to the west.

In modern history we have had changes in religious music. Many church choirs have picked up the tempo so common in black churches. The Catholic Church has introduced the guitar and other instruments to the altar. The fundamentalist church Assembly of God use a full orchestra and four singers with microphones to lead all the singing. All this has been accepted in varying amounts, but in most churches the hip-hop or rap is still sacrilegious, because it may not be teaching good moral decisions. It is the same with the majority (but who can count) objection to the swing beat to the National Anthem. Many of the old hymns from the 1600s are just too difficult for the average voice because they are too complex, not sung often enough and the majority can't read notes so the parishioners just mouth the words or wait until it is over. In early America, singing societies were formed for social reasons but more importantly to learn to sing by notes. This was very popular among the Germans. However, this generation will not live long enough to hear a Missouri Synod Lutheran minister utilize a little rap music to make a serious sermon more palatable to young people, because to some churches it would be like asking the devil to assist with the service. During weekend musical festivals, the Sunday morning gospel singers have big, appreciative audiences and many of the attendees have never attended an organized church. In the music world there were fifty thousand Christian and Gospel albums/singles sold in 1999, while they sold 175,000 R&B but only seventeen thousand classical. There are more and more crossovers of the categories but the black music heritage and southern gospel is very popular.

A serious problem has existed for at least three decades, which faces many churches of all denominations in the inner city. As an isolated example, the Bushnell Congregational Church in Detroit was a landmark, with a very large facility and active members. The inevitable happened during the migration to the suburbs, the results of which were obvious when the parishioners left. Those that stayed behind were mostly older people, and in many cases some were driving ten to fifteen miles from the suburbs to attend services. It was also obvious that the finances to maintain the church facilities exceeded their income due to the decline in membership. The soul wrenching decision had to be made to move in the direction of the parishioners. The church split with some diehards remaining but most would move and start the Meadowbrook Congregational Church. They now have a new younger congregation of families living close to the church. The new Sanctuary and church growth was mainly due to the progressive and dedicated work of Dr. Neil Hunt. Stopping this trend is far from a religious solution, it requires the rebirth of the inner city.

Last but not least it should be noted that religious freedom was the catalyst for not only exploration but free enterprise as well. With religious freedom came free enterprise and Laissez Faire (no government control except for defense and property rights). Democratic government through revolution would follow. The spark of revolt or the courage to improve one's position in life can be traced to the Protestants replacing illiteracy with reading skills to verify what they had come to believe as sacrament or is it sacrilegious. They could determine for themselves what the Christian bible says or means, but they also continued reading the works of a continuous parade of philosophers who wrote of democracy, or the untenable lot of the peasants, and the tyranny of the kings. Serfdom would end with the mindset to create a better controllable existence even at the cost of martyrdom of the few. Many philosophies failed. The commune format of the little Plymouth Colony, which was later advocated by Hegel, Marks and Lenin, failed. Free enterprise won, and the taste of freedom was good. To be able to elect your own leaders was right. The direction was established, but unfortunately the Christian religion not only opened the floodgates of freedom, but also opened Pandora's Box for religious diversification beyond control. Getting organized by Christianity involved but a few basic concepts or religious beliefs from which all the present denominations grew. This was in light of the fact that it was 1776 before the world population reached one billion and in 1919 it grew to two billion, but in 1999 the population reached six billion. Such rapid growth in recent years had a disproportionate influence on religion.

Chronology of Chapter VIII

1611	First Presbyterian Church in America was organized in Jamestown, Virginia.
1611	Thirty Years War starts in Bohemia.
1620	English Puritans arrive at Plymouth Rock.
1639	Roger Williams starts Baptist Church in America.
1642	English Civil War, Puritans & Presbyterians versus Anglicans & Catholics.
1643	Presbyterians dominate Westminster assembly, write Directory for the worship of God.
1646	English Parliament establishes Presbyterianism as state church.
1647	Quakers founded in England, also called Society of Friends.
1648	Peace of Westphalia ends thirty years war.
1685	Edict of Nantes denying Protestants rights causing Huguenots to flee France.
1689	Act of Toleration in Great Britain gave rights to dissenters.
1700	Baal Shem Tov creates Hasidism (ultra conservative). Jews are freed from the ghettos.
1701	Act of Settlement forcing all British Kings to become members of the Church of England.
1706	Presbyterian Church is established in America.
1707	Philadelphia Baptist Association brings together churches in Pennsylvania, Delaware and New Jersey.
1721	Russia eliminates office of Patriarch and establishes church administration as an office of the government.
1720	Great Awakening Revival in America.
1729	Methodist movement in England by John Wesley, an Anglican priest who started the Holy Club.
1729	Moses Mendelssohn translates Torah into German and opens the First Jewish School.

Chronology of Chapter VIII
(Continued)

1755	Synod of Constantinople denies validity of all sacraments of Roman western church.
1755	The Baptist Church is started in the South during the Great Awakening.
1763	The start of the Seven Years War.
1764	Brown University is started by the Baptists.
1768	First Methodist Church in America.
1775	Start of the American Revolution.
1781	Last executions by Spanish Inquisition.

9

1800–To Date

❖

Modern History Of Denominations

In the final history chapter, which was a period after the Revolutionary Wars of America and France, the Revivals are the newsmakers of the day. William Miller, preaching from a Baptist pulpit, accused of being a fanatic, set dates for the Second Coming of Christ. The first date, March 21, 1843, did not produce his expected results, so he set a new date, October 22, 1844, which was eventually called the great disappointment. It was a quiet, normal day. He set no more dates, but his followers started the Seventh Day Adventist Church.

One of the most influential voices opposed to slavery came from Henry Beecher, from the Congregational Church in Brooklyn, New York. Later he fought for women's rights. As his outlet he published the non-denominational journal called the Christian Union, which later became the Outlook in 1870.

Dwight Moody, a Unitarian, was converted to a Fundamental Evangelist in 1856 and in 1860 joined the Young Men's Christian Association. He is most noted for his efforts with Ira Sankey in promoting the gospel hymn. He is said to have preached the old fashioned Gospel, opposed the so-called social gospel, evolution, and supported the literal translation of the Bible. In 1879 he founded what is now the Moody Bible Institute.

Billy Sunday was a former baseball player who became a Presbyterian minister in 1903. His forte was Evangelism and he became a Fundamentalist following in the footsteps of Dwight Moody. His greatest prominence came in the campaign to prohibit liquor but he failed to stop the booze from flowing out of Chicago. Some estimates run as high as 1 million converts who came forward in his meetings to be converted to Christ. He was considered by many as a sensationalist.

This brings us to our present day Evangelist, Billy Graham, a Fundamentalist who is respected and loved by most. He used the radio, tent revivals and the Youth for Christ Movement to reach millions. Starting with his visit to the White House to visit President Harry Truman, he became a regular visitor to the Presidents of the United States. In 1996 he was awarded the Congressional Gold Medal.

As religious history has unfolded, there seem to be approximately thirty-six denominations or religions that have the majority of followers in a broad spectrum of theologies. They are as follows:

DEISM: The American Revolution was instigated and led by young, wealthy patriots who like the successful Puritans in Plymouth, sought other religious outlets, instead of a public display of gratitude to God for their success. The result was a concept that came out of the Age of Enlightenment called Deism. I think it is best that I quote from <u>Britannia</u>: "The proponents of natural religion were strongly influenced by three intellectual concerns, a growing faith in human reason, a distrust of religious claims of revelation that led to dogmatism and intolerance and finally an image of God as a rational architect and an ordered world." The deist, and I quote again "applied the scalpel of reason to much of the piety and practice of Orthodox Christianity itself. They reject the elaborate liturgical practices and complex institutional trappings of Roman Catholicism as analogous to ancient pagan superstitions." The deist wanted to view religion as a religion of reason, but deism itself was not a religion. The best explanation of deism was demonstrated in a lecture at Wayne State University in Detroit, which explained that God created the earth, gave it a big spin, and forced it into an orbit about the sun, and established its natural laws. From then on God was finished and left the world to operate according to rational laws.

Deism was moderate in England and Germany, but in France the corrupt Roman Church priests caused a reaction and a bitter attack from the deists. Voltaire said "every man of sense, every good man, ought hold the Christian Sect in horror." For many of the French philosophers deism was a short cut to atheism. It is claimed by historians that in America most of the leaders of the revolution, signers of the Declaration of Independence and the Constitution were Deist. It may have been that the first three presidents of the United States were Deists.

ROMAN CATHOLIC CHURCH: In the reformation the Roman Church was attacked by its own Augustinian Monks for, as Britannica states, "corruption and lack of spiritual vitality." After the start of the reformation the Roman Church called the Council of Trent, which consisted of twenty-five sessions over twenty years, and was concluded in 1563. The main accomplishment (in addition to eliminating the indulgences) was to clarify the church position in regard to the Protestant justification by faith alone, and the authority of the scripture alone. The Roman Church hammered out the doctrinal view that justification is by faith, but also by works, which they based on scripture and tradition. They also confirmed the Latin Vulgate, which the Protestants discarded as far as scripture is concerned, and the Protestants would only acknowledge the original Hebrew, Greek and Aramaic text of scripture.

The French Revolution was a very difficult time for the Roman Church. In 1790 the collaboration between the Revolutionists and the Roman Church ended. Anti clerical accusations broke out and most of the bishops, fearing for their lives, fled from France to Italy, Germany, Spain and Switzerland. In 1791, the revolutionists split with Rome and started a cruel movement against the church. The underlying reason for this violent approach was that the revolutionary committee discovered that the Roman Church owned over half of the land in France.

This placed a double burden on the French peasants in that over half of the land was tax-free and they had to pay higher taxes. Taxation had been increased to the point of driving the peasants to revolution. The increased taxes were to replace at least in part, the money donated by the French to the American colonists for their revolution. By confiscating the church land, they could use the land as collateral for the revolutionary committee to borrow money. The attack on the church was called dechristianization against the Roman Church, and finally against all Christianity. During the infamous "reign of terror" all public worship was forbidden. Any priest who resisted compliance (out of the few who remained in France) was arrested and liable to be put to death. One hundred thirty priests were shot to death in Lyons alone. They closed the Protestant Churches as well, and abolished the Georgian calendar so as to remove Sundays from the week. The Jacobins, as the revolutionists were called, were led by the most radical leader of the reign of terror, Maximilien RobesPierre. There were a few conscientious people and undercover bishops in the National Convention who started religious services in secret, until in 1794, separation of Church and State brought the priests back into France, which was and is a predominately Catholic country.

The next official re-evaluation of Church tradition came with a Vatican Council in 1870, called by Pius IX, which produced the two most important wedges that were driven between the Roman Catholics and the Protestants. The first was the creation of Infallibility of the Pope. This was in reaction to the Church fear that the age of reason and enlightenment with the Darwinian theory in particular, would distract from the authenticity of the Bible. The second was the dogma of Mary, which pronounces that Mary lived her entire life without sin, and that Mary, through intercession, had the most or greatest influence with God. Prayer to Mary became an integral part of the Mass.

These two concepts didn't find support with the older priests in Germany, a Catholic area. They rejected them outright, and refused to convert their church teachings and burned all of the previous texts and material. They were called the "Old Believers," located in the Netherlands, Germany and Switzerland.

In addition to these two wedges, the Pope condemned freedom of religion, freedom of speech, civil marriages, and secular education, etc., in what was called the Syllabus of Errors (eighty negative points) of the modern time. The Syllabus was a statement of retreat from the modern world. The doctrinal differences are still based on the veneration of the sacraments. As we discussed earlier, Luther and others only accepted two of the seven sacraments of the Roman Church. Luther felt that only Baptism and the Eucharist were biblically based. The Roman Church has seven sacraments based on tradition. They are, baptism, eucharist, marriage, penance, holy orders, confirmation and anointing the sick. In addition, they include the tradition of intercession or seeking spiritual help through the saints and revering the saints, especially Mary. The private confession didn't start until the eleventh century and confessional boxes appeared in the sixteenth century.

The Council in 1870 reaffirmed church authority but unfortunately the church didn't recover their losses in Europe but the church grew in the New World. History shows that leading up to the First Vatican, it was the dedication of the dynamic Jesuits that revitalized the church. They not only reached the New World with the explorers and built missions to establish permanent roots, they also established schools in Europe and gained support from nobility. They made the church international.

In 1962–65, the second Vatican Council by John XXIII is said to have attempted to strengthen their doctrinal presentation in the wake of many questions and divisive followers. After the council, the mass changed from stressing of the saints and praying to them, to stressing the Eucharist in the mass. Without getting into the theology of the last council I find that converting to English (or the vernacular of the area) from Latin to English in all the masses was in one way, for a short time confusing. The priests were accustomed to quickly saying the Mass in Latin because no one understood the words anyway. When they did the same in English, it was almost inaudible. They soon slowed down and turned the altar around to face the parishioners. There are only a few churches that still offer at least one mass in Latin. When Pope John Paul II was questioned about errors in the 1870 council he said "you can't use today's mentality to judge the facts of 150 years ago."

It is interesting to note that converting to English did cause one very unique situation. There were non-Catholics and atheists who attended when the mass was in Latin and enjoyed the solemn beauty of the church but they didn't understand the Latin words which they would not have agreed with.

There are one billion Roman Catholics, with 60 million in the US and discounting the fact that many millions are in very poor countries, with most of the people never having known anything else, they have always enjoyed and benefited from the beauty and solemnity of the mass itself. The church still has internal problems. Some estimates run as high as eighty-five percent of the church faithful do not follow church edicts, particularly in birth control, and most disapprove of celibacy. When it was reported that new recruits to the Priesthood dropped from twenty-seven thousand to seven thousand the seriousness became obvious. The Roman Church, however, has always made the necessary adjustments to remain the largest church on earth.

Last but not least, the effort of Pope John Paul II to start the healing process of past differences with the Lutherans, Anglicans and Jews is a significant contribution to religious understanding. His apology for the inquisition and for ignoring the Holocaust took great strength of character. However, there is still much to be done.

The Chaldeans, Eastern Rite of the Roman Church, are in even more serious trouble. There have been 120,000 who immigrated to the Detroit area from Iraq and surrounding areas, and fifty thousand born here since 1920. They have six Churches and not enough priests to service them. To make matters worse, in a recently published report, they only have one priest in training who will not become a priest until 2003.

ORTHODOX CATHOLIC: The Orthodox or ecumenical patriarchate of Constantinople was created by 50 AD and was characterized by their antiquity and the pomp and splendor of their form of church worship. They were formed along with four other patriarch centers in Jerusalem, Antioch, Alexandria and Rome. The Greek Orthodox Hellenistic Church is the only Christian church claiming decendency from a Hellenistic background. Hellenists were in general Greek speaking Jewish Christians. There are those that don't consider them Christians, just Greek speaking Jews. They were referred to as Grecians. Greek influence was strongly felt in both Jewish and Christian faiths. Actually there were very few Jews that converted to Christianity with the most in Alexandria. Since the East and West churches went through the whole series of councils together, I will leave the explanation of the original aspect of the Orthodox Church to the theologians.

In the fourth century, Constantine moved the Roman government to Constantinople. It is interesting to note that the Roman Church patriarch stayed in Rome all during the period involving the fall of the Roman government to the barbarians. Very soon the east and the west churches started drifting apart. Rome claimed the dominant position but really created the schism when as we have reported earlier, the Filioque clause accelerated the rift into the threat of separation. This clause is very important because it is an omen of things to come. The church will forever split over interpretation. The clause Filioque added to the Nicene Creed by the western church, "I believe in the Holy Ghost, the Lord and giver of life, who preceedeth from the Father and Son, who with the" etc. The Orthodox version is "I believe in the Holy Spirit, the Lord and giver of life, who preceeds from the Father, who with the" etc. There are those who consider this hair splitting but this is a theology debate and it is certain that political supremacy gave an impulse to the dispute. When the fourth crusade in 1054 CE sacked Constantinople, the schism became permanent.

The icons were the second divisive theological point of contention. It was not until 887 CE when the eastern church officially added icons to their altar, providing a beautiful, rich ceremony with the formal paintings of Christ, of Mary, and of many of the saints. The West felt that because Christ was, for a time, a human man, it did not justify divining human nature. They and all other Christian churches in varying numbers, claim it is close to idol worship. Particularly the Protestant churches who stripped their altars and some even removed the cross. The Roman Catholics, Lutherans and Anglicans often have statutes or images of Jesus and perhaps a painting of the Last Supper. Most churches accept stained glass windows. The new Catholic churches have become very plain, with a beautiful building, but an austere altar.

The Eastern Church maintained the Patriarchate in Constantinople in the period called the Byzantine Empire, but did not claim the individual authority of a Pope. The early church literature was in Greek, but by the fourth century the West had adapted Latin. From then on it was the Latin West and the Greek East. In the period after Russia was converted to Greek Orthodox, a balance existed between East and West. Soon after, however, the West gained territory and power, especially after Constantinople fell to the Muslims to be the Ottoman Empire in 1453 CE. Russia became dominant. The Ottoman Empire recognized the patriarch of Constantinople with authority over the Eastern Church. Russia, in 1593, became autocephalous (independent patriarch). So also did Greece in 1833, Romania in 1865, Serbia in 1879, Bulgaria in 1870, and Albania in 1937. The Eastern Church lost the beautiful cathedral of Hagia Sophia to the Muslim forces, so the small church of St. George served as cathedral for the patriarchs.

There was confusion after the Russian revolution and the American churches were cut off from the Russian church. The non-Russian ethnic groups formed separate jurisdictions with their Mother Church. The patriarch of Constantinople also formed a Greek Archdiocese. The creation of an Autocephalous Orthodox Church in America in 1970 gave permanent status without dependence on any foreign control or ethnic origin. The two main groups not involved are the Greek Archdiocese and the Ukrainian Orthodox Church.

Historically speaking and perhaps over simplified, it would seem that for a few words in the Nicene Creed, a misguided Fourth Crusade, and a few paintings on the altar, the Catholic Church could have stayed united. The Roman Church has quite conclusively proven that the Pope's system of control has worked successfully, except for the Reformation, proven by their count of one billion members.

In 1998 the Georgian Orthodox Church withdrew from the World Council of Churches, claiming that the WCC didn't consider the Orthodox on an equal basis with the other 330 members. Also in 1998 the Russian Orthodox Patriarch Aleksey II refused to meet with Pope John Paul II based on what the Russian Church claim is an irreconcilable difference that has to be first settled by ground work laid out in lower levels. It has been said that only ten percent of the Russian people ever attend church.

METHODIST: In England the Methodists first break with the Church of England came in 1795. The first Methodist body was called the Methodist Episcopal Church, and was started in 1834. Within a century of the death of John Wesley and his brother Charles, missionaries had been sent to almost every country in the world. They assigned more and more responsibility to laymen and promoted women to the level of preachers. Wesley's instruction "press on to perfection" was not realistic for later generations. The emphasis on a strong local control and organization, and the use of lay preachers provided a platform for expansion not only in England but also in America, where it was the largest denomination. The circuit riders followed the western frontier and were the main catalysts in this growth. In 1844 the growth was interrupted by Civil War which divided the church into north and south. They were not reunited until 1939, at which time they joined the Methodist Episcopal Church North and South, into the Methodist Church. In 1969 they merged with the Evangelical United Brethren Church to become the United Methodist Church.

Methodists took missionary work world wide, with strong administration, connecting and controlling the clergy and lay preachers. The faith of the believers to transfer ones personal life to Jesus and the church has dominated this worldwide movement.

Their love for the singing of hymns started with Charles Wesley who wrote many of the most powerful lyrics coming out of the eighteenth century.

HOLINESS MOVEMENT: Continuous schisms produced many Holiness and Pentecostal denominations, which grew from the Holiness Movement. The Pentecostals have never merged into one common organization or belief. They differ among themselves in all matters, particularly in the form of worship.

In 1867, in New Jersey, the National Association for the Promotion of Holiness was formed. During this time, the Church of God was formed and soon after the Church of the Nazarene was formed from two of the Holiness groups. They have basically been a gathering of the poor or poverty stricken, left out of the middle class. This can be seen in the storefronts, tents and small wooden buildings used for services. The traditional denominations rejected them, but many have been very successful in the world of electronic preaching by such charismatic preachers as Oral Roberts, Jimmy Swaggert, Jim Bakker and Pat Robinson. They have, since the 1960s, attracted followers from all denominations. An attempt to bring back spiritual holiness led to the forming of the Church of the Nazarene, the Assembly of God and many others.

While we're on the subject of charismatic preachers, somewhere along the line the term "born again" came into prominent play among many of the Fundamentalists. It started with the conversions, which required the participant to come forward and publicly announce his or her faith in God and/or the parameters of what the congregation established as proper acknowledgment of faith. This was common with the early Puritans. Today, however, the charismatic preacher, with the open Bible in hand, exclaims that unless you are born again, in that moment, at that place, you may not make it back to your home safely that night. Eternal damnation in burning hell is the only alternate to being born again. This I have witnessed as far back as my youth, by attending tent meetings of traveling evangelists. I have seen people, mostly women, come forward, then roll on sawdust floors because they were so inspired by the Holy Ghost and claimed they were born again. On the part of the born again individual, a kind of hypnotic spell occurs which penetrates the brain and propels euphoric, glorious feeling of relaxed peace with God. The trouble is that it is mostly temporary and can be carried too far for the benefit of someone other than God. Jim Bakker went to jail for misusing millions of dollars, some of which was sent to him by poor widows, money which they could hardly afford.

This is a good place to bring up diversity of interpretation of the bible. I do not intend to interpret the bible, but can point out how individuals differ on the way they translate the passages. It is very sad that individual churches can reveal exact meanings of statements in the bible, which actually can be taken out of context or misinterpreted. For example, in John 3 verse 3 it says that "you must be born again to see the Kingdom of God" but in the next verse 4 Nicodemus asks how is that possible, which is answered in verse 5 which states that "you must be born of water and the Holy Ghost." This is interpreted by most churches that Jesus is referring to baptism.

Some preachers demand "say amen" or "raise your hands and say I believe," but I don't find this in the early church. Jesus' Sermon on the Mount was a process of teaching. There does not seem to be any record of people shouting or coming forward to pray for seventeen hundred years after Jesus. This all comes down, however, to the fact that religion is a faith and we all have a God given right to believe as we feel in our heart. It is historically true that many faiths must condemn others in many ways through segregation, prejudice, fear and even war. The basis of this book is to search historically, how we have managed to come up with so many faiths and the lack of respect for others.

UNITARIANS: There were those, however, that swung the pendulum all the way to the left. They were the Unitarians who kept no synods or councils, presbyters, creeds, catechisms, or fathers of the church.

Every man is destined to stand on his own faith. They reason that all of the above would limit free thought and a creed written by one man would not necessarily be the creed of another. After all, they contend Jesus and his disciples never wrote a creed and historically creeds have caused wars and schisms. They also contend that the Bible is good but not infallible. The Unitarians and their associates, the Universalists, are in their words, grateful to science for eliminating or dispelling degrading or harmful superstitions and myths. The American Unitarianism was also affected by Arminianism. This was a liberal schism from Calvinism, named for its leader Jacobus Arminius, a Dutch theologian. This liberal movement, which continued into the Methodist faith, also influenced John Wesley. Only twenty-five percent of Unitarian members are Christian which is the result of having no creed. Each church can create their own path to follow. It should be mentioned that there is a small group called the Unitarian Universalist Buddhist Fellowship.

CONGREGATIONAL: The theology of the Congregational Church, and its position in general terms, is between the Presbyterian and the Methodist, and what would be considered non-fundamentalist Baptist. It stresses each congregation should make its own church decisions without a higher authority and as Luther taught, the priesthood of all believers. In the sixteenth through the eighteenth century, the Congregational Church in England grew and fell several times until 1906 when the labor party gained strength. At this time they reached their highest position. Soon after, a majority joined with the Presbyterians to form the New United Reformed Church in England.

They had much more success in the United States starting with the Pilgrims seeking a new approach that would generally liberalize their day-to-day lives. A more radical movement changed some Congregationalists into Unitarianism. Soon after, however, the great awakening gave the church a substantial boost. Some members merged with the Christian Church and the Evangelical and Reformed Church to start the United Church of Christ. The name Congregational still exists as such, worldwide. They stress a personal experience with God, accept two sacraments, baptism and communion (they offer communion twice a month). They also stress the sermon or teaching over the reliance on scripture.

The National Council of Congregational Churches was formed in 1871, but enlarged in 1931. In 1961 they merged with the Evangelical and Reformed Church to form the United Church of Christ.

LUTHERANS: The Lutherans in America came with both the Orthodox tradition and the Pietism of the continent, but not the enlightened rationalism. They came first to New York, the Carolinas and Pennsylvania in the 1740s. They came with several languages other than English so they moved into isolated rural communities and contributed very little to local politics. It became evident that they were contentious of each other as they formed into synods. The influence of Samuel Schmucker was to Americanize and join with the Reformed Evangelical Churches. Another group wanted to maintain the Lutheran Synod. Carl Walther, who formed the Missouri Synod, led the most militant. He did not allow Lutherans to commune and pray together unless they were of the Missouri Synod. Many suspicions were cast that the Germans would not be loyal during World War I so they purposely set out to be Americanized. Sermons were at least partially given in English and the confirmation classes were for the first time conducted in English. After 1918 most Lutherans, 5.5 million joined three synods to form the Evangelical Lutheran Church of America (ELCA). The largest non-ELCA group was the Missouri Synod with 2.5 million members. The ELCA was formed mostly in the North, around the states of New York, Pennsylvania, Virginia and the Carolinas. The Missouri Synod basically is in the upper Midwest. The Wisconsin Synod, still smaller and more isolated, started a series of parochial schools to protect their youth from public education. They forbid any association with other groups if prayers were given. This they feel is tantamount to accepting their beliefs. They forbid membership in lodges and Boy Scouts. As an example of how many Lutheran Synods were in existence, the Lutheran Church of America was formed in 1962 from the American Evangelical Lutheran Church, the United Lutheran Church in America, the Augustinian Evangelical Church and the Finnish Evangelical Church, all of which merged into the Lutheran Church of America. In 1988 the Lutheran Church of America joined with several other Lutheran Churches to form the Evangelical Lutheran Church of America (ELCA).

After World War II, Lutherans had become more national in scope. The Missouri and Wisconsin Synods still consider themselves Orthodox Lutherans. ELCA (approximately 6 million members) and the Episcopal churches (3 million) are at least discussing the merger or sharing of each other's clergy, sacraments, cooperation in mission projects, and making joint decisions on major issues. The hold-up was in the Lutheran objection of the basic selection of bishops in what is called "historic episcopate." The Lutherans have never utilized this system which involves the installation of new bishops by three established bishops. This is considered as maintaining a continuous orientation existing from the original Apostles. This is a method of selection of bishops in the Catholic and Orthodox churches and also the Episcopal and Anglican Church. These discussions do not involve the Missouri or Wisconsin Synod, who are not inclined or even receptive to any changes.

In 1999 the Lutheran World Federation in Augsburg Germany signed a resolution with the Catholic Church to resolve the dispute, which was the reason for the reformation in the 1500s. This action and the discussions with the Episcopal Church indicates that the Lutherans are anxious to combine forces to manage more efficiently the training of ministers, combine missionary work and increase influence in the local areas. More than one hundred ELCA Lutheran Churches in the Detroit area agreed to bless gay unions, which is opposed by the National Lutheran Church.

BAPTIST: The Baptist Church was first formed in 1631 and from the beginning in America, didn't appear to be a serious schism from the Colonial Puritans. They are more an American development but the terms Particular Baptist and General Baptist first appeared in Europe. The difference had to do with whether atonement was for the select few or for all believers. The Particular Baptist prevailed as a sizable force in the middle colonies of New Jersey, Pennsylvania and Delaware. The Philadelphia Baptist Association started a missionary program that spread the Baptist area from the Carolinas to Connecticut. The growth was again as in other churches, part of the Great Awakening. The numbers are impressive when you consider 494 Baptist Congregations grew to 1,152 during this time. In 1814 they added baptism by submersion and the newly adopted theory that only adult believers can be baptized. At that time they also started publications, education and home missions. It took nearly two hundred years, 1639 to 1814, to formulate the beliefs of the Baptist Church. The Church would face a major schism in 1845 with the differences in the question of slavery. Combining all the Baptists today may number 30 million. As in most religious membership totals however, they are divided into many groups.

SOUTHERN BAPTIST: The Southern Baptists began their own programs of missions and education. It was not until 1907 when the divisions of territory were established, and finally the American Baptist Church in the USA brought together all of the older groups and allotted territory. The Southern Convention after World War II moved across the whole country and became the largest Protestant body in the USA (15.5 million). After World War II the Baptists dedication to youth programs and materials furnished by Sunday Schools, grew in numerical strength, soon passing all other Protestant Churches.

The latest influence to the Southern Baptist movement came from conservatists at the convention in 1979. In 1990 the right wing took complete control and took the SBC into the political arena in the Republican Party. Their views were dominant and had been stated by several sources as "no room for difference of opinion." They demanded a word for word inerrancy of the Bible, total submission of a wife to her husband and for their program to set up a missionary drive to convert Jews to their belief in Christ as the only way to salvation. The success or future ramifications of this program would best be discussed with a Rabbi from the Messianic Jews, and is beyond the scope of this book. They also outlaw abortion, gays and women preachers. The forming of an opposition group is gaining support but news reports indicate that this involves only two thousand churches out of forty thousand. A very large number of Texas members have on their own voted to disregard wifely obedience, but still remain in the SBC. In a Time Magazine report "Battle of the Baptists" by David Van Biema, he refers to the theology dispute within the Baptist church as hair splitting. Those who believe that accepting Christ is the main criteria of their faith openly oppose the word by word belief (literal translation) in the Bible. Christ provides a more personal relationship with God and a bit more room for interpretation of the Bible. The inerrancy of the Bible won out at the last convention but storms are on the horizon.

Other Baptist churches are the National Baptist Convention with 2 million members and the Progressive National Baptist Convention with another 2 million members. The latter in 1961 became spearhead of the Civil Rights Movement under the leadership of Martin Luther King, Jr.

BLACK CHRISTIANS: By 1700 the slaves born in the United States outnumbered those being brought in by slave ships. By 1750 to 1800, both Methodists and Baptists were preaching to the blacks. The great revival also had a tremendous influence on the black community. The Presbyterian Church as well as the Methodist and Baptist, sought out blacks but they had to sit in separate pews in the rear of the church, or when possible in the balcony. Both whites and blacks practiced the same tradition and liturgy. Black preachers became more available, which brought on and introduced black congregations. The blacks often had separate and hidden services in the back woods. This resulted in self-expression or a separate slave religious mentality, which has been referred to as a free vent of emotion. By 1816, a black Methodist preacher organized the African Methodist Episcopal Church. The Civil

War and liberation did not really help or change the religious tradition of the blacks, they were still faced with poverty, lack of education and racial prejudice.

After the Federal troops left the south in 1877, the blacks were, as some have said: "put back in their place." It was reported that in the 1890s, there were three lynchings per week. The church now played a very important role. It provided hope, acceptance and dignity. The growth of these churches was amazing. By 1900 practically every black child was a member of a black church. It was their social center. The black churches were bible believers rather than evangelical. They were spontaneous, free to respond, and had a close relationship with the preacher. Many sects and cults resulted, one of which was led by Father Devine, 1879 to 1965, who claimed to be God incarnate.

When you hear the joy and the very happy music of the black churches, it is easy to realize religion was all they had to cling to for so many years. In the eyes of God they were equal and they sang "Hallelujah." They have many more free churches and remain biblical oriented.

From the black churches came the civil rights movement led by Martin Luther King, Jr., representing the Southern Christian Leadership Conference. He made permanent changes in the black's fight to gain equality without resorting to violence. This resulted in the Civil Rights Act of 1964. Unfortunately, like so many great men, he was killed by an assassin's bullet in March 1969. His oratory will forever be an integral part of black history. At the Washington march the phrases "I have a dream" and "I have been to the mountain top" plus "Free at last" will guide the black movement on a non-violent but relentless course.

DeBois founded the NAACP in 1909. Another group of black activists stressing non-violence was formed in 1933 by Elijah Mohammed called the Nation of Islam (Black Muslims). They claim biblical precedence and teach black equality and request monetary compensation from the United States for their enslavement of three hundred years. One of their requirements for membership is to change their surname. This was to symbolize the reversal of their name change on the slave ships when the captain, who could not spell or pronounce the African name, gave them new simple names. A modern example is Cassius Clay, the boxer, becoming Mohammed Ali. Elijah's main spokesman was a former prisoner, Malcolm X. He had studied history and religion in prison and had a strong aptitude for public speaking, which was the one aspect of the Islam movement that Elijah did not like. Malcolm's rhetoric slowly changed to advocate violence, so he was removed from the Nation of Islam and formed the Muslim Mosque to continue his movement. Other radicals assassinated him in 1965. Elijah said of Malcolm "He taught violence and died from violence." Malcolm had a large following who felt his cause was just and violence would be necessary. Elijah died in 1975. Louis Farrakhan, who organized the "Million Man March" in March 1995 in Washington, DC, carries on the movement of Islam. The Nation of Islam still follows it's divine Minister Louis Farrakhan, who teaches the words of Allah to unite all humanity where all people can enjoy peace and the brotherhood of man. The Nation has deteriorated into what may be just a mirage.

REFORMED: The Reformed Church dates back to the Dutch Settlement in New York (then New Netherlands), which was the established Church of Holland. It was completely controlled by Holland with preachers from Amsterdam. The Colonial pressure forced a division in the church between the loyalists to Holland and the new self-governing Reformed Church in America. The large migration from Holland in 1850 increased their church rolls with most of the immigrants settling in Michigan. They had tried but failed to unite with the Presbyterians.

PRESBYTERIAN: The Presbyterian Church was originally the Reformed Church in Switzerland and Southern Germany. In England it took the name Presbyterian due to the self-governing format of the elders (Presbyters), who were elected by the congregation. The struggle in England regarding the government of the church was from those who wanted to keep the Episcopal (bishop) form of the Church of England, and those who wanted the Elders. In America the Elder system was adopted and the Presbyterians became a major church of the Reformed Movement.

MORMONISM: Mormonism had its creation during the second great awakening with revivals that covered most of the states in 1830. Joseph Smith, Jr., in an open field in the countryside of Upper New York, was said to have received a revelation from God on two gold plates. His contention is that Jesus Christ appearing on earth, had given the prophet Mormon the truth on two gold plates which had been buried, not to be revealed for 2400 years, at which time Smith was told where they were buried. The engraved record, which Joseph Smith translated, became the Book of the Mormons. It is revealed that only Smith could read this because he had been provided with special eyeglasses that translated the ancient language. He contended that the angel who gave him the plates was named Moroni. The story, which the plates revealed to him, was that a group of Hebrews came to America in 600 BCE and established two clans or groups. The Laminites forgot their heritage and became the American Indians. The other groups, the Nephites, built a great civilization but were annihilated by the Laminites.

From strictly a rational point of view, the story possibly could have been started by Smith who was totally involved in the revivals instead of just going out to preach, and felt he had to back up his new ideas (like Moses on two stones) by receiving them on gold plates. In order to explain how they got to Upper New York, the story of the Hebrews was sufficient. The plates were old and the printing would not have been in English so he came up with the special eyeglasses that automatically translated for him.

Regardless of the creation of Mormonism, it is today a Christian, God fearing dynamic group of 4 million members. Their beliefs have changed over the years. Their polygamy is now illegal, but it is known that there are isolated cases of multiple wives in Utah. It is often explained that Mormonism is a combination of Jewish, Christian and Smith's ideas. The most important difference (we certainly don't want to get in too deeply) is that the trinity is three separate persons. A person's salvation depends on conducting his own life, with Baptism on behalf of the dead, that God was evolved from man, and that the young people are asked to give twenty four months of their lives to Missionary work at their own expense. Smith did not end the possibility of adding canon. He acknowledged that the future presidents of the Mormon Church would speak for God. Their revelations must be accepted as divine law or canon. Historians found indisputable evidence that John Smith and members of his family had been involved with folk magic and a cult religion, which has raised serious and troubling questions about the revelations of the creation of Mormonism.

After Smith organized a devoted following, he moved the group to Kirkland, Ohio. Unfortunately they were facing armed rejection by the local people, so they moved to and founded Nauvoo, Illinois. This area was no better and Smith was arrested by the locals for being a fanatic leader of a group in their territory. While in jail, a mob broke in and killed him and his brother Hiram, on June 27, 1844. Brigham Young took command to move again, but this time on a one thousand mile trip to Salt Lake City. The first group consisted of 143 people but was soon followed by one thousand or more. One more interesting point is that the Mormons used irrigation successfully for the first time, to farm in desert conditions. They applied for statehood but until they stopped practicing polygamy they were not accepted. In 1890 when they promised to change their customs of polygamy, Utah became a State.

Members who disagreed with Smith and eliminated many of the more radical departures from Orthodox Christianity created the Reorganized Church of Jesus Christ of Latter Day Saints. Their headquarters were set up in Independence, Missouri. Joseph Smith, a son of the founder was president from 1860 until 1914. It never grew to equal the numerical numbers of the Mormons of Salt Lake City.

CHRISTIAN SCIENCE: Christian Science was created during a period of Darwinism and with questions regarding the authority of the Bible. Mary Eddy Baker, in 1879, based on her own ill health, questioned God's responsibility for human suffering. She found there was a middle ground between what she called stern Protestantism and doubtful liberalism (Unitarianism). Her quest for answers was increased through her own experience with alternative healing and homeopathic medicine, which followed many years of study of the scriptures. She wrote extensively about science and health, which she revised over time to become the "Textbook" for the study and practice of Christian Science. Mrs. Eddy and her followers founded the Church of Christ Scientists in 1879. She wrote the manual of the Mother Church, which gave direction and success for her Church. The Church stresses reading the Bible and provides Reading Rooms for this purpose, with a strong emphasis on Jesus' healing. By 1930, there were 2,400 churches with membership near 300,000. There has been a slow decline in membership as in most churches in recent years. Some criticism has been unfair because they do encourage the use of dentists, optometrists, and physicians when needed. They also comply with all health laws and inoculations. They do pray for healing and as we have noted, in faith healing there is a phenomenon associated with the brain, that if convinced in a believable way, will assist in the healing of the body, which oftentimes medicine and physicians cannot do. This is faith. They have, however, recently been sued for two million dollars (with Supreme court approval) for the death of a boy for whom medicine had been withheld in favor of prayer. This does seem to be an isolated case.

ADVENTIST: The Adventists (means coming) believed in the imminent coming of God, or the return of Christ as promised in Revelations of the New Testament, as well as the end of the earth. In a way, all Jews and Christians are Adventists, but there is a degree of emphasis. The Christians called Adventists created the Pentecostal Church, Jehovah's Witness, Fundamentalists, and Seventh Day Adventists (the largest of the Advent Group). The Seventh Day Adventists conclude from the Old Testament that God rested on the seventh day. They are very sincere, however, that the body should be God's temple and should not be abused. They follow strict rules regarding drugs, alcohol, coffee, and some eat no meat. Other Adventist groups are Evangelical Adventists formed in 1845, Adventist Christian Church in 1860, Church of God in 1866, and all agree on the Second Coming of Christ.

In historically tracing the authority or Biblical history of the Seventh Day Adventist's Saturday worship service, we find that in the Jewish history of the Old Testament, it is more than likely that the author (designated only as "J") had borrowed the concepts of a seven-day week. This may have been taken from an earlier period (the Bible story was not written until approximately 800 BCE). Long before the Bible story was written the Sumerians and Babylonians in Mesopotamia divided a week into seven days, during which they designated one day for rest and recreation. It was not until 321 CE, a thousand years later, that Emperor Constantine established the seven-day week in the Roman calendar and designated Sunday as the first day of the week and the day of rest and worship (he had been newly converted to Christianity). The history of the calendar itself is difficult to follow because there is the Roman Republic calendar, the Julian calendar and the Gregorian calendar. In addition there are many more, such as the Babylonian, Greek Metonic, Egyptian, Chinese, etc. Historians admit it is difficult to pinpoint any events by today's date or calendar. As an example they can only come within seven to ten years of the actual birth of Jesus. It is historically difficult to understand how a church can determine that God rested on Saturday, when all the other religions agree with Constantine's suggestion and all celebrate on Sunday.

SHAKERS: The Shakers are in the same general category as the other Adventists, and were formed in approximately 1650 in Manchester, England. The Shakers would be overcome with emotion and actually start to shake during service, hence their name. They arrived in the

United States in 1770 with a small number of followers. Their popularity was the highest in 1870, but has since reduced in numbers to almost non-existence.

ISLAM: The World of Islam can best be described as one dynasty after another. The one aspect, which resulted in an international Islam, is that even in the conquering days, they did not force the Muslim religion on any of the conquered people. Remarkably, many converted to Muslim in many different countries.

The most significant division in the world of Islam, even today, is the Shiites, and the Sunnites. Eighty-five percent of all Muslims are Sunnites, or the Sunni branch of Islam. They are considered Orthodox.

One of the main stumbling blocks to a United Islam is that Shiites believe the ruler of the Mosque or Imam (holy man) must be in a line of decendency from Ali (son-in-law of Mohammed) as they interpret the Koran or Mohammed's own instructions. The Sunnites believe that the law gives the people the right to select the ruler of the Islamic society. The Shiites point out that Mohammed set down the rule for eating and washing, and would have laid down the method of selecting their leaders. They take words out of the Koran to prove their point but the Sunnites disagree and prove their point from the same material and therein is created the schism. The Shiites exist mostly in Iran, but perhaps there are 100,000 in Saudi Arabia, a large portion in Iraq, perhaps a third in Lebanon and a small number in Pakistan. They still only represent fifteen percent of total Islam.

We, of course, remember when the Iranian Ayatollah Khomeini (Shiite-Imam) declared the United States as the great Satan. The American hostages whom he imprisoned fell in the category of prisoners of war. They could be imprisoned or ransomed (never killed) as long as the war went on, a war that Ayatollah felt he was verbally conducting. This was a problem for the USA in that they were up against fanatical elements that claimed we were evil because we had aided the Shah (the former ruler). The USA was attempting to find friends in the volatile area of oil rich countries. If the US had declared war and invaded to free the prisoners there would have been a million Shiite martyrs. The US decided to wait it out and the prisoners were eventually released. Now that the Ayatollah has died there is no Imam alive, but they anticipate the arrival of one.

The required pilgrimage to Mecca called the Hajj continues for all Muslims in greater numbers and is unique. It is a mass commemoration of the story of Abraham and his obedience to God and being willing to sacrifice his son Ismael (not Isaac as the Jews claim). The rite must be performed once a year and until 1945 was a great physical ordeal. The main devotion takes place at Kaaba, Islam's chief shrine, located in the center of the great Mosque in Mecca, which is the size of two modern day football fields.

The pilgrimage starts by first arriving in Saudi Arabia and changing clothes to the traditional garb of the Hajj. For men this is one sleeveless white wrapper for the upper half of the body and another for the lower half, mostly with one shoulder bare. Women wear full-length white dresses and no gloves or veil, which are forbidden. The dress contributes to the sense of the communal body. The Handbook of Hajj, which is prepared by Islam teachers, says a big rush and some confusion is natural when hundreds and thousands of people assemble. They make every effort to perform ceremonies and make movements in their calm and quiet way. The calm, however, is not always the case. In the years that Hajj falls in high summer, the heat is relentless and very difficult for the elderly and handicapped. The program goes on for ten days and is much too complicated to go into detail here. Not every year is smooth, as in 1987 when a struggle between Shiite pilgrims from Iran provoked a fight with Saudi security forces, which resulted in 400 deaths. Saudi is proud of the normal pilgrimage and security, which they provide. Heads have rolled for individuals causing interruptions. In 1945 the pilgrimage was 37,630 strong. By 1980 the number reached 2 million, coming from every continent. There are approximately 1 billion Muslims. It is one of the fastest growing religions in the US with 6 million faithful.

Within the Shiites and Sunnites there are several important groups and sects that differ in unique ways. The Sufist are described as mystics and base their deviation from Orthodox Muslim on love and mysticism. They developed a more personal approach to God and are more closely related to the common people. The term for its members is Dervish (Arabic), which resulted in the term "whirling dervish." They had introduced music and dancing which was foreign to Islam. They also had prayer beads copied from the Catholic tradition of using the Rosary. Most of the religious details had been secret, so little was written about them until as late as 1970. Due to their popularity in Egypt they have made a noteworthy contribution to the history of Islam.

Wahhabism is the modern reaction to the superstitions and mysticism of the Sufis and their worship of holy men and holy places. Mohammed Ibn Abd Al-Wahhab first introduced the theory. He was a Jurist (lawyer) who was raised in surfism and later rejected their ideas. Thomas Lippman in <u>Understanding Islam</u> states "he started a public campaign against the rights of the mystics and of the folk-religions, against worship at tombs, prayer to holy men, minor pilgrimage, and belief in Mohammed's intercession with God and initiation rituals." Wahab taught that the basic concept of Mohammed, the Koran and God was still the modern Islam. He influenced and was joined by Mohammed Ibn Saud in 1740 and later by Abdul Azizibn Saud, the ancestor of the first king of Saudi Arabia, Abdul Aziz. The forces of Abdul Aziz had great expansion success until the Ottoman Sultan, with support from Egypt, drove the Wahhabs back and captured their ruler and executed him. Wahhabism still exists and the House of Saud was to be saved by an exiled young prince, who with a tiny band of forty men won decisive battles in recapturing Saudi Arabia, and established the first King of Saudi Arabia, Abul-Aziz.

A very important part of Muslim history was the struggle between the Hashemite ruler of Mecca, Abdul Aziz and the Wahhabi forces.

Hussein was successful in his revolt against the Turks and made an alliance with the British and French. Unfortunately, the British and the French double crossed him and colonized the whole area. The battles with the Turks and the Caliph are best remembered as the desert campaign assisted by British officers and T.E.Lawrence (Lawrence of Arabia) in particular This was followed by the overthrow of the Ottoman Turkey into a secular republic and eliminated the Caliphate. The betrayal of the British and French reduced Hussein in power and prestige. In 1926, Abdul Aziz was proclaimed King of the Hijaz. In but a few years all the tribes of the peninsula were incorporated into the Kingdom of Saudi Arabia. It is important to realize that Abdul Aziz returned Islam to the Arabs and stopped the Turkish influence of corruption and cruelty.

The Druze is a small sect living in Lebanon, Syria and Israel. They are ultra moral monotheists, who were Shiites. They seemed to just blend in, not discussing or openly seeking converts. They are in the middle of the Israeli Palestinian struggle but don't get involved.

The Alawites are the rulers of Syria. President Hafez-El-Assad is an Alawite and rules Syria with only eleven to twelve percent of the population as members of the sect. They have been oppressed by the Turks, the French, and hated by the Sunnites. Outsiders rarely understand or care about Alawitism because they are very secretive. Egypt has opposed the Assad politically but they hang on to power with a strong military. They always face a diversity of faith and tradition, and there is also a strong Christian element.

The Muslim Brotherhood which Lippman in <u>Understanding Islam</u> described as a political rather than a religious organization, is dedicated to a whole Muslim state. In the brotherhood, religion and the state are inseparable. They terrorized Syria and the Assad rule, which resulted in their being outlawed. At one time there were twenty thousand slaughtered in Syria.

It is unfortunate that so many disasters and incidents have not only prevented a solid Islamic front, but have seriously undermined the reputation of Islam. The United States watched with great concern, the Iranian revolution in 1978–79, which was immediately followed by the war between Iran and Iraq. The literal destruction of Lebanon, the bitter struggle between the leaders in Afghanistan, Palestinian struggles and finally the Iraq invasion of Kuwait in 1990 all show a lack of political cohesiveness in the world of Islam. Terrorism breeds strange individuals with a warped concept of Allah. Bombing of the Pan Am Jet flight over Scotland in 1988, which killed 270 people, mostly Americans, cast a shadow over Islam. It was terrorists in 1993 who bombed the World Trade Center in New York.

On September 11, 2001, terrorist Osama bin Laden, born of a wealthy Muslim family, whose beliefs are a serious deviation from the teachings of Mohammad, perpetrated the most disastrous concept for killing Americans by sending two fully loaded aircraft to fly into and destroy the World Trade Centers in New York, resulting in the death of more than three thousand people and billions of dollars of destruction. The Pentagon in Washington, D.C. was also attacked by another plane and a fourth was brought down in the fields of Pennsylvania. The world, including Muslims, was in total disbelief at the atrocity and is trying to understand, apprehend and eliminate terrorists who have no respect for human life.

A united front of just the Arabian Muslims is inconceivable at this time. This is especially true when you consider the number of groups, some fanatic, involved beyond just the Shiites and Sunnites, or within these groups which cover such a diverse concept of religion and government. There are many more sects over the years that have gained support but have faded away. It is not understood exactly what is Mohammed's teaching and what must be done to adjust to the changing technology of the modern world and to reestablish itself after being freed from Colonial rule of Britain, France, Holland, Italy and Russia. Being under Colonial power (which itself could be an interesting study of government) did not change the Muslim religion but did bring modern technology to a desperately poor people. Iran and Saudi both outlawed satellite TV but they can't outlaw the Internet. They are educating women, so what will their attitude of women be in the future? A good example of the progress of Muslim women is that they have a woman Prime Minister in Pakistan although they are not Arabian Muslims.

The Islamic world today has an internal dilemma within themselves, exaggerated by modern technology after the days of colonization. Today's countries were often formed by a line drawn on a map. The overall consequence has been that today you could not be sure that any government would be the same tomorrow. The Islamic determination that the government must comply to the world of Allah through his messenger Mohammed, recorded in the Koran, the Hadith and the Sharia, presents the problem that there is no throne or Caliph, no one to set today's rules. The example in Afghanistan is that when the Kabal government leaned toward the left, Muslims fought Muslims. That brought on the Russian army, which resulted in the Russian Vietnam. This poor country literally destroyed itself. In Iran the church felt that the Shah became immoral, and he was replaced with an Imam (holy man), who created for the United States, the term, the "Great Satan." Here again, the outlawing of satellites, as in Saudi Arabia, stopped technology. Technology will continue to invade all of the Islamic states. It took a coalition of nations to put Iraq back into its borders. Kuwait appreciated the help from the United States, but disliked having foreign troops on their soil, especially women.

President Sadat of Egypt was assassinated for making a peace treaty with Israel. This was carried out by another fanatic group called "The Society for Atonement." They objected to rock music, alcohol, and dancing, which they defined as immoral. Mubarak of Egypt has had many of his government people assassinated and is still fighting to bring Egypt out of poverty. Power plants and technology are in the future.

Albania has ripped itself to pieces where forty thousand people were killed in a short period of time, during an internal strife. Indonesia,

Pakistan and Nigeria are also cited as being in bitter struggles trying to define themselves.

BAHA'I: The youngest new independent religion. This is a splinter group, which was formed as a schism of the Shiite Muslims in Iran around 1844. The founder was Mirza Hozeyn Ali Nuri who claimed to be the Imam (Messenger of God). He was called the Bab. His strongest exponent was Mirza Ali Mohammad of Shiraz Iran. He spread the faith to North America and Europe and his is the sacred literature of the Baha'i faith.

Most of the Baha'i faith is concerned with social ethics. They believe in one God who created the universe but who is unknowable. The Bab declared that all of the leaders of the great religions were manifestations of God and that there must be a unity of all mankind. Baha'i accepts Abraham, Moses, Zoroaster, Krishna, Buddha, Muhammad and Jesus as messengers of God. They strive to reduce racial, class and religious prejudices. There are no sacraments and no clergy, they restrain from narcotics, alcohol and practice monogamy. It is interesting to note that they had their own calendar with nineteen months and with nineteen days each. Each local assembly participates in electing a universal house of justice (located in Haifa, Israel) to govern the 5 million international Baha'i.

HINDUISM: By the fifteenth century Hinduism reached a theistic plateau, but still within the Brahmanic Orthodoxy. Much of this theology is from the Bhagavad-Gita, the most important and influential text in India. It is actually a condensed and perhaps revised version of the Upanishads. The developments of two sects are important to note. One is the Caitanya, which was noted for its hymn singing, dancing and parades. It is the modern interpretation of the Society for Krishna Consciousness or as we know them, the Hare Krishna. The second was created by Guru Nanak and recorded by Guru Gobind Singh, to produce a new religion called Sikhism.

By the twentieth century many reforms were instituted in Hinduism, which abolished many of the old cruel practices, particularly in regards to women and child marriages. The Bengali mystic Ramakrsna introduced the elements of change in the west. Jnakirama Vithala of the Bharatiya Temple in Troy, Michigan informed me that it was Vivekananda, a student of Ramakrsna that really introduced the Hindu religion to the United States. He gave the address in 1893 before the World's Parliament of Religion and made a very good impression on the group. He also introduced the Vedanata Society. It was Janakirama Vithala who later gave the address before the Parliament of Religion in Chicago. Vithala was kind enough to allow me to study in the Temple library. The people in his office refer to him as Sastoy, which is a nickname given because of his lengthy name.

There are 750 million Hindu followers in the world, including 1 million in the United States, and the numbers are continually growing. Vasham's <u>Classical Hinduism</u> points out that the future of Hinduism is assured because of its adaptability. They always maintain the classical Hindu thought and practice, although the members can adjust to their place and time. Hinduism will remain one of the world's great religions. The enormous Hindu Festival Purna Kumgh Mela lasts for six weeks in the Holy Merging Rivers of the Ganges and the Yamuna, near the city of Allahabad. This includes more than 30–40 million pilgrims who come to absolve their sins and prepare themselves for the life hereafter. The holy men wearing nothing or a small loincloth lead the process of marching into the river. The latest twelve-year cycle fell in January 2001.

JAINS: The Jains (the non-violent vegetarian branch of Hinduism) built a new Temple for the one thousand Jains in Farmington Hills, Michigan in 1999. Bhupendra Shah of Northville, Michigan, is the board chairman of the new Temple, which stresses their dedication to not killing a living thing, not even an insect creeping into the house.

SIKHISM: Was created by Guru Nanak in Punjab, India, in 1469 and recorded by Guru Gobind Singh in 1699, who according to Basham in <u>Classical Hinduism</u> combined elements of Islam and Christianity with Hindu theology to produce a new religion called Sikhism.

It is found worldwide today. Their Holy Book established an equality, which eliminates the Hindu Cast System, and any form of idolatry plus complete equality between men and women. They also stress feeding the poor and welcome the public to join them. There are 20 million Sikhs world wide, with a half million in the United States. The men still wear turbans, although it is not required except in the sanctuary. In recent years in Punjab, India (northwestern India) they have been very successful and prosperous at growing wheat and started to demand political advantage. This brought a military assault by the Indian army that killed thousands of Sikhs. In 1984 two Sikhs, in retaliation, assassinated the Indian Prime Minister Indira Ghandi.

JUDAISM: In reporting on a modern Judaism it should be noted that there are two developments to forever change their basic tradition. First, in Europe, following the Middle Ages, the Jews moved out of their ghettos and were given more tolerance and in most cases were offered citizenship. Scattered as they were, the Talmud was their guide and reference. The Jews were, as time progressed, acquiring a sense of nationalism for which Webster gives the definition "a sense of national consciousness exalting one nation above all others." This nationalism gave the Jews an impetus, a driving force to have their own nation. The term for this is Zionism. It would not be until after World War II, that Palestine was subdivided to create Israel. It was seriously felt by the new state planners that Palestinians, who lived there and called it their home, would blend or be absorbed by surrounding Arab nations. Unfortunately, this was not to be. The Palestinians were pushed back into temporary quarters and would till this day demand a piece of territory to establish a Palestinian state. In the Six Days War of 1967, Israel proved they were a modern well-equipped army, and gained more territory. It didn't end there as the Israelis and Palestinians kill, murder, ambush and fight continually. Peace Treaties were made impossible as long as the Palestinians would not recognize Israel as even existing, and were dedicated to its destruction. It seems that now that the Palestinians have recognized the existence of the Israeli state, that Israel must give up and give the Palestinians a state of their own. Israel was first created with 600,000 Jews, which today has grown to 5 million, with 2.5 million that have immigrated and the balance born in Israel. Most people in the US don't realize that one of the serious deterrents to peaceful coexistence with the Palestinians is in the very complicated religious makeup on both sides. Not only are the Jews divided three ways or more, there are Jews that do not follow the Jewish tradition. In addition there are many Palestinians of several traditions that have always lived in Israel. On the West Bank there are many Palestinians that are not Muslim. There are Arabic Christians, Coptic Orthodox Christians, etc. In Jerusalem the city has a Jewish section, Christian section, Muslim section and the Armenian Orthodox Christian section. This is not conducive to peaceful coexistence

The US has financed and supplied Israel with military aid, which makes it the best-trained and best-equipped army for its size, in the entire world. It must be acknowledged that the US is giving Israel billions of dollars a year, not entirely for charity. In so doing, they create an extension of the US Army in an oil rich, most important powder keg. No one should be surprised at the animosity and fighting because it has been going on for thousands of years, back to Ismael and Isaac. Islam and Judaism both consider Jerusalem their Holy City, so it would seem that it would always have to be an open city or free city. There are many wealthy Jews in America that will provide funds as long as Israel needs help.

The second influence for change to the Jewish tradition is the advancement of technology and social change. Many Jews feel that they no longer live in the ancient world, and must make allowances by changing some of the basic oral traditions. They have created three Jewish faiths or institutions of religion. The Reformed Jews believe in living with modern conditions and lifestyle. The Orthodox are of course determined to adhere to the law, profits and customs of the Jewish tradition. The third group is somewhere in between, called Conservative. It seems that it was the Jews moving west in the frontier days, being isolated from their traditions that created a more compatible reform movement. The Jews that came from Europe later were mostly Orthodox. At the present time, the Orthodox represents forty-five percent while the reform represents twenty-one percent and the conservative thirty-four percent. Conservative Rabbi Dea Wyler of Germany was the first woman Rabbi, which is strongly opposed by Orthodox Jews.

One more point about the Jewish faith is the dietary laws. The tradition holds that they can eat no pork (in the early days it caused trichinosis due to unclean handling). All meat must be quickly and neatly slaughtered so as to prevent blood from remaining in the meat. The conservatives hold to most of the dietary laws, but the reform eliminated them based on the new modern sanitary conditions. The word kosher means that the Rabbi has inspected the food and declared it clean according to his standards. My only experience is with milk; when a rabbi came to the creamery and after inspection allowed the creamery to apply a kosher label on a sufficient number of bottles to cover the Jews in that area. The creamery had to pay him five cents per bottle for his approval.

Another component that was imported from Eastern Europe is the American Jewish establishment called the Hasidism, which was developed by Mordechi Kaplin, and called reconstructionist. He approached Judaism ideologically and practically, or as a historic way of life, rather than God given laws. This approach would be considered the left wing of the conservative movement. Another component or group and by far the most radical are the Messianic Jews. They are small in numbers but believe that Jesus is the Messiah. The group would at least resemble the first Christians who were Jewish followers of Jesus. One local group met for religious observances in a rented Baptist church.

There has been, as with most churches except the Fundamentalists, a decline in organized Jewish church life. Membership and attendance have both declined. Even though they have a decline, and many follow a secular life free of orthodox discipline, they still demand a Jewish communal religious identity and its institutions, but live free of the Jewish traditional restraints.

There are only 24 million Jews world wide, and no religious group has suffered more over such a long period of time. It all started with forty years of roaming around in the desert, captives of the Egyptians, Assyrians, Babylonians, Persians, and Alexander. Finally under the Maccabees they built a nation that they lost when the Romans burned the temple in 70 AD. This scattered the Jews world wide with only the Talmud to guide their faith. After the torture and holocaust at the hands of the crusaders, they gathered into ghettos throughout Europe. After finally getting citizenship in many of the cities, the greatest of all their misfortunes finally came in Germany with 6 million souls destroyed by Adolph Hitler in World War II. This event did contribute to the creation of Israel and finally a homeland. Wars and border killings have continued to this day, for a God fearing devoted people of high morals, but a persecuted people in every sense of the word.

The most current event in Israel in addition to the Orthodox refusing any form of peace with the Palistians, is their fight to keep the conservative or the reform women from praying at the west wall or wearing the prayer shawl. After a long struggle the supreme court ruled in favor of the women, but with the control of the parliament the extreme orthodox immediately passed a law forbidding women this right and adding a seven year prison sentence if the new law was violated. When women approach the wall they are hissed at by Orthodox women and called things like "you are as bad as Christians and Muslims." Historically, if one recalls how many times the Orthodox Jews were hated, one might wonder if this is self-inflicted. But this discussion is beyond the scope of this book and we can only pray that peace can come to the area soon and the killing stopped.

BUDDHISM: Buddhism was spread by missionaries (Sangna) who settled first in Sri Lanka around 300 CE. By 1800 CE Buddhism had risen and declined, but gained substantial strength again by 1900. The

Pali-Canon was written in 100 CE in Pali, which was the ancient dead language.

In the eleventh to the thirteenth century Buddhism was introduced in Burma and even during British occupation, 1885–1948, it survived and is said to have developed its own style of meditation.

In Thailand the Thai Buddhism is under partial state authority. It is strongest and has more adherents in the countryside.

In Laos it is another matter. The war in Vietnam in the 1970s seriously halted Buddhism but today the Sangna Buddhists are negotiating with the communists.

Indonesia had the highest Buddhist population, but with Islamic pressure, they have experienced a decline. According to John Snelling's <u>Buddhism</u> there is a modest effort to revive both Theravada and Mahayana Buddhist traditions. India, Pakistan, Afghanistan and Central Asia, were once the trade routes, but there were more than material items that flowed through these routes. The spread of ideas, technologies and philosophies, which included Buddhism were spread to the most remote corners of the world. Korea became a permanent Zen Buddhism tradition but it too is in decline.

Japanese royalty accepted Buddhism from the beginning. The highest level of popularity came during the Samurai who established the Shogunate or military power. The Zen, with their strictness, suited the Shogun. Japan developed its own version of Buddhism called Shinto. The people, however, are often both, as proven by the fact that weddings are often Shinto, but funerals may be Buddhist, in the same family. The Shinto Temple has a much simpler architecture, which is a contrast to the beautiful roofs of the regular Buddhist Temples.

I was fortunate to accompany a Japanese industrialist to a Daianji Temple in Sakai City in Japan. This is a Rinzai Temple that dates back to 1300 and one of the two major Zen Buddhist sects. The Rinzai is divided into fifteen sub sects of which the Rinzai Tofukuji owns the Daianji Temple. My translator, Kaji, kept me advised as to the ceremony involved for our visit. Also accompanying us was our Japanese associate. Kaji informed me that our visit to the sanctuary is most uncommon, and was due to the large contributions to maintain the Temple, by our host. The entrance hall completely surrounded the Temple. The walls of the halls were beautifully decorated with artwork, which have been designated important cultural assets by the Japanese government. The paintings are of birds, mostly cranes, and beautiful wisteria and other blooming trees. Inside the outer wall was a series of meditation rooms with sliding doors. The sanctuary, which may not be the right terminology, was in the center, where we sat in a row on very thin pillows. The Monk obviously in charge, sat facing us and spoke at length to our host. This was followed by the entrance of four monks, each carrying an ornate bowl four to five inches in diameter, and containing a dark green liquid. They knelt in front of us and gave each of us a bowl, after which they stood and exited. The first monk turned and faced the corner of the room and a large cabinet (the only furniture in the room) and gave a recitation that sounded like poetry. Kaji whispered in my ear that this was a very great honor and on signal be sure to drink the contents of the bowl. I did, and the taste was strange, but as instructed, I finished it to the last drop. There was much bowing and smiling as we left. The ceremony was dedicated to our safe travel and that we would soon be home. Each Shinto Temple can have their own ritual or vestments. In this Temple the significance of providing food or nourishment was for our travels with the Temple's blessing. In 1945 Japan created a constitution with freedom of religion. This ends the Buddhist and Shinto as state religions, and many other religions have flourished.

    Buddhism was introduced to Tibet around 700 CE but it was 1000 CE before it established itself. As more Monks came from China, they established both a Monastic (Monasteries) and Tantric Buddhism (Yoga and Mystic, a part of Vajrayana). Tibet became, as Snelling, in his book <u>Buddhism</u> points out, "the custodian of the hallowed tradition of Chinese Buddhism with a new tone or color." From here it spread to Mongolia and Russia. In the US during the last century Buddhism provided a need especially by young people who were not satisfied with the materialistic trends in religion. Intellectuals introduced it in Eastern US, Great Britain and Eastern countries. In the Western U.S, they came via the Chinese railroad workers, as did Hinduism. The Chicago World Parliament of Religions offered a springboard. The Parliament was addressed first by the Zen Master, Soyen Shaku, in 1893, whose pupil was Suzuki, a leader of Buddhism in the US.

Zen Buddhism is differentiated from Buddhism in dependency. The pure Buddhist depends on Buddha for enlightenment, but the Zen Masters in 1700 taught reliance on oneself. Put another way, in Buddhism, man could not save himself and relied on Buddha. Zen on the other hand, taught that man must save himself. The mind is a reservoir that contains man's mental ability to save himself or strive toward self fulfillment. According to the Zen Master, there is no other place to seek salvation except oneself. As a result many feel Zen is less a religion and more a way of life.

The 2–3 million Buddhists in the US have the same problem as Hinduism, in that changes must be made to assimilate women into the mainstream. They must also change to accommodate freedom and democracy, as contrasted to their former feudal laws. Thich Nhat Hawh, working in France, came up with the expression "Engaged Buddhism." Hinduism and Buddhism are both growing in the US but must keep abreast of individual thought and practice. The brand or style of Buddhism developing from their considerations is the "Nichiren Sho-Shu" or the true Nichiren School. This is the form embraced by some movie and sports stars, and the like. It teaches that one must first control and guide oneself. Destiny is established by yourself and you must take responsibility for your own life. In Buddhism there is no absolute or single God but rather that the mind is the creator, so therefore you are your own master.

In the most recent news regarding Buddhism in Tibet, the CNN News reporter David Turley, spent time in Tibet and interviewed the fourteenth Dalai Lama, who is considered the head of state in exile received asylum in India when the Chinese government invaded and controlled Tibet in 1957. Most recently the Dalai Lama visited the United States and discussed possible cooperation with the Chinese and his return after forty years in exile. He is also discussing democracy, which is now possible in Tibet. The Dali Lama also explained that it would be wrong for his followers to worship him as a God King or as a living Buddha. He is only a Buddha Monk with knowledge about the Buddha Dharma, who can relate knowledge, beliefs, views of the Dharma, and discuss reincarnation.

A small group in the United States refers to themselves as Esoteric Buddhists. They have several in the United States with the Dharma Center in Asheville, NC. The leader John Wu is also associated with the Nectar monastery, which is the US Outpost of the School of Buddhists.

Other small groups exist today, even under communistic control, such as the Naxi (pronounced Nah-Shee) in southern China. It involves approximately 250,000 followers and Dongbas (priests or translators of the ancient text). This again is a religion of right living.

Falun Gong is a Chinese spiritual system of exercise and meditation and is strictly a spiritual movement of the 1990s. In China the communistic government is fearful of this group because there are signs that they are bigger in numbers than the communistic party itself. Their growth is phenomenal when you consider the opposition of the government. They have no buildings or for that matter no infrastructure. They have no actual clergy and they follow a practice called Quigon (Chee-gong) that does not have a belief in God but stresses a unity of all life in the universe. They pursue three goals; truth, compassion and forbearance. It is a purification of the mind or a state of peacefulness. Although small in numbers they have a following developing in the United States, it is mostly Asian, but in Germany for example, half of their numbers are Germans.

MORAVIAN BRETHREN: We discussed their origin in the last chapter and their relationship with Lutherans, Pietism, and Armenianism. Of the Moravian immigrants seeking religious freedom, some went to England and a larger group to America. On the boat to Georgia in the US in 1735, when Wesley was visiting America, he discussed and exchanged ideas with his newfound friends. On his return he and his brother joined the meetings of the Moravian Church. Each went their own way by 1740 and the Methodist Church expanded exponentially, while the Moravian Church became a very small church in America. They settled in Georgia but not successfully and soon moved to Pennsylvania and the Carolinas in particular. They built schools and trained preachers. Some of their communities were closed much like the Mennonites and the Amish. They have a synod which met every ten years to determine all doctrinal matters. Communion is given in most cases, six times a year, but in a few cases once each month. They utilize both the Apostles and the Nicene Creed.

SALVATION ARMY: In 1865, William Booth organized the Salvation Army in London as an Evangelical group to benefit the poor and the homeless caused by the Industrial Revolution. It is Evangelical but utilizes a military structure. Most units organize a band and often march to their meetings in uniforms. Their effort in helping victims of disasters and wars is greatly appreciated and world known. They operate in approximately eighty countries. The officers in the Salvation Army are the same as preachers in the Protestant Church. Women are considered equal to men in all respects. The Army is always thought of as an open religion, with singing and instrumental music and a call for repentance and conversion.

In 1896, Ballington Booth, one of William Booth's sons, a National Commander in the US, split with the Salvation Army over disagreements, particularly in the area of military structure. He set up the Volunteers of America, which is still very active with headquarters in New York. It is smaller and is an entirely different organizational structure, but maintains a very respectful and charitable program.

AMISH/MENNONITES: You can still see the horse and buggy of the Amish in Lancaster County, Pa., Northern Indiana, Central Michigan and a few other areas. They base their beliefs on the early Christians or before individuals like St. Augustine established church doctrine four hundred years after Christ. They do not follow the lead of Constantine who built the first church building in the fourth century, and meet in each other's barns for service and business meetings. There are some kinks in their armor of the otherwise strict Amish Canon. There are examples of ladies in some groups wearing a light pastel cloth for their dresses in lieu of the austere black, which is traditional. When the ground is too hard to plow with horses, some have utilized tractors. They are still industrious and take advantage of the Amish facade that what they grow or produce is a better product. I once talked to an Amish gentleman who revealed that their products were as good but not necessarily better, so they get a higher price because it is Amish. They accept the additional price gracefully. The elders strictly enforce their rules of conduct. Punishment for an error can be shunning, which is a process of isolation for a period of time but still within the group. If someone marries outside of the church, they are faced with expulsion. It will be interesting to observe future advancement in their austere life. There are dairy farms that now have electricity to operate the milk parlors, so does this mean we will see an untrimmed, bearded Amish farmer with his black hat and buttons instead of zippers on his trousers, looking at the Internet to get stock prices? There could be even more changes but by maintaining the isolated community they are not faced with day-to-day pressures of the outside world.

SCIENTOLOGY: For our purpose in this book, we will briefly mention Scientology because we cannot determine if it is a religion. It was first established in 1954 and their first magazine was published in 1968, called Scientology. L. N. Hubbard started the movement. They want to be called a religion because churches do not pay taxes. It appears to be a pseudo psychiatric attempt to affect the brain in such a way as to provide a clearer outlook on life. It has been criticized for the large amount of money demanded and received for their diagnostic and therapeutic practices. Several Hollywood stars are involved. The US government is still investigating them.

NATIVE INDIANS: The Native American Indian religion dates back hundreds of years. It is not possible without volumes of research, to cover the five hundred cultures and 250 languages of the American Indians at the time of Columbus. It was estimated there were 50–70 million Indians in the Americas, with 10 million in what would be United States territory. Many cultures and traditions have come and gone, but basically they used every day life for natural resources to establish oral tradition. They associate faith or prayer with growing food, hunting and fishing and day-to-day living. They have rituals for thanksgiving and for blessings, etc.

One of the traditions that caused a problem was the use of Peyote (a hallucinogenic drug from the cactus plant). It was known for at least one thousand years and was used long before the Spanish conquest of Mexico. The Spanish and the Jesuits condemned it. The Franciscans in 1680 raided the pueblos, destroying the Kivas (village ceremonial centers), where the use of drugs was alleged to cause uncivilized dances and ceremonies. In 1882 the Secretary of the Interior, Henry Teller, ordered an end to heathen dances because they were not conducive to civilizing the Indians. In 1978 the American Indian Religious Freedom Act was passed, but forbid the use of Peyote. Many dances still remain, such as ghost dance, the green corn dance, and the sun dance. The supernatural is reached through the Shamans or the medicine men. The false faces of the Iroquois are used to cure diseases or possession by evil spirits. Other drugs such as made from the Jimson weed were used to obtain visions and used, for example, at the celebration of the young boys doing the puberty dance. The Indians have always had great respect for the elderly and hold their gravesites as sacred. The traditions and customs are still followed but in many cases the influence of their recent successful gambling casinos may have had a modernizing effect. A recent US law mandates the returning of religious items and the confiscated bones of sacred burial plots to the Indians. To study the history of the first inhabitants, archeologists had used the bones for research.

CULTS: There are cults that accumulate their membership (victims) for personal gain and mostly from inexperienced youth seeking something that is missing in their lives, with dreadful results. I am in no way referring to the Christian movement of Billy Graham who for so many years has brought people around the world to Christianity. I am referring as an example, to the Jonesville Camp where a preacher named Jones convinced a large group to give up all their personal wealth and belongings to go to Jonesville, Uganda. This is where he so warped their minds saying that the government was going to outlaw their church that he convinced the whole group of nine hundred people to commit suicide and follow him to heaven.

The current growth rate for Christians is not in mainstream formal churches but rather in livelier and indigenous churches such as the new "Restoration of the Ten Commandments." A former Roman Catholic apparently created this. The event that brought this group to light was the mass suicide by three hundred to five hundred Christians who had been convinced the earth is going to end and it seems they wanted to get ahead of the crowd. The regrettable aspect is that those people had been convinced to sell their homes and donate everything to the commune. Further, in most cases if it does not end in suicide, it will end when the charismatic leader leaves with all the money or just ahead of being arrested for sex offenses. Simon Robinson reporting for Time Magazine lists additional Uganda cults as "The Holy Spirit Movement" (a violent sect). "The Lord's Resistance Army" (used children for soldiers and sex slaves), and "The World Messenger" were disbanded by the police for rape and murder. Equally as frightening is the current case of two grandparent couples fighting in court to adopt the three children whose father and mother, on different occasions, were killed by snakebites, in a church which used snakes to prove their faith. The maternal grandparents are members of the same church where the parents died and the paternal grandparents are not. Where is the dividing line across which the local authorities will step in to say enough? But then I am writing about the history of religion, not its idiosyncrasies.

The report in California on the Jesus People, a cult, offers more questions than answers as to why so many do not trust an organized church. They present Jesus as a long haired revolutionist who rebelled against established religion and the political environment. Their contention is that he fought for criminals, prostitutes, street people, and the poor. One must admit that Jesus did forgive the criminal on the cross, his right hand assistant was Mary Magdalene, a former prostitute, he did help in healing many people on the street, and he did say that the poor people would inherit the earth. Why the Jesus people and other such groups put their trust in some charismatic individual who is out for his own gain or power instead of an established, legitimately organized church is a question that defies answers.

Another cult called Heaven's Gate felt that their leader, a minister's son, would lead them to terrestrial life as aliens, being delivered by space ships. No doubt drugs and alcohol helped in the illusion, but unfortunately thirty-nine members committed suicide so that they would be ready when the space ship arrived. How very sad.

Chronology of IX

1800	First Methodist camp meeting.
1801–75	Zacharias Frankel founds Conservative Judaism, a compromise between extremes of Orthodox and reformed Judaism.
1801–1917	Violent attacks against Jews in Russia, mass emigration to US and Palestine.
1830	First Methodist Protestant Church established by reformers.
1814	Society of Jesus refounded (Jesuits).
1814	Congress of Vienna.
1840	Two Irish Synods unite to form Presbyterian Church of Ireland.
1843	Wesleyan Methodist Church founded by abolitionists.
1844	Methodist Episcopal Church split over slavery.
1844	Baha'i Religion was created in Iran.
1845	Potato famine forces many Irish Catholics to flee to America.
1845	Southern Baptist Convention splits with General Convention over slavery, plus doctrinal and procedural disputes.
1870	First Free Methodist Church is formed (conservative).
1847	Churches in Scotland unite to form United Free Church of Scotland.
1854	Doctrine of Immaculate Conception of Mary is declared by Pope Pius IX.
1858–61	United Presbyterian Church of North America was formed, but slavery issue split off the Southern Presbyterian Church.
1869	Dogma of Papal Infallibility.
1872	Start of Jehovah Witness Church.
1875	Various branches of Presbyterian Churches unite to form Presbyterian Church of Canada.
1878	Christian Science Church is formed in Boston.
1884	Russian Baptist Church is organized.
1890	Buddhist revival in Japan.

Chronology of IX (Continued)

1896	Billy Sunday, Presbyterian evangelist, attracts big crowds.
1900	Diocese of Aleutian Islands and North America is established in San Francisco.
1905	Baptist World Alliance is founded for Missionaries in Asia, Africa, Europe and Latin America.
1908	Union of Evangelical Christians is formed in Russia (4.5 million Baptists by 1927).
1915	Armenians massacred.
1917	British Government supports Jewish state of Palestine.
1920	End of Ottoman Empire.
1922	Russian Bolsheviks seized all church treasures.
1925	In Canada, Presbyterians, Methodists and Congregationalists merge to form United Church of Canada.
1933–45	Holocaust in Germany.
1939	Methodist Episcopal Church, Methodist Episcopal South, Methodist Protestant, form one Methodist Church.
1948	State of Israel is created.
1955	Presbyterian Assembly approves ordination of women. Methodists do likewise.
1953	Pope Paul VI and Constantinople Patriarch Athenagoras abolish the Anathemas of 1054 and reestablish communication.
1967	Six Day War—Jews capture Jerusalem.
1972	Presbyterian Church of England merges with Congregational Church of England and Wales to form United Reformed Church.
1979	Fundamentalists gain control of Southern Baptist Convention from Moderates until 1988 when Moderates regain presidency.
1989	Presbyterian Church membership fell to 2.9 million from 4 million.

10

To Date

❖

A Changing World

As we conclude our trip through the history of religions and observed the many schisms on the way, we realize it has resulted in some tumultuous times. We still have religious intolerance where we should have love. We should have respect for other people's faith. Schisms should be replaced with mergers. One answer to all this is pluralism, which is defined in Webster's dictionary as "a state of society in which members of diverse religions will maintain an autonomous participation in and the development of their culture or special interest within the confines of a homogenous community."

Religious pluralism has been a recent topic for discussion for a rather new organization called "The Ecumenical Institute for Jewish-Christian Studies." The executive director is David Blewett. I have attended their meetings and find these very enlightening, educational, and witnessed the dedication to harmony by Rabbis, Roman Catholic priests, Protestant ministers and religious educators. They publish a booklet on protocol for visiting other than your own churches, to attend weddings, church services, funerals, etc. This group is oriented to relationships and non-conversionists.

Another activity, which we attend, is the Interfaith Prayer Service each Thanksgiving. It is a service in which each of the participating religions offer a prayer in their own tradition. The last one was held at the Islam Wisdom Center in Dearborn, Michigan, and the previous one was at a Jewish Synagogue. The host church or synagogue conducts it, with a Rabbi, Priest, Protestant Minister, Hindu, Muslim, and a Baha'i Priest giving a prayer of Thanksgiving. I find them very interesting and proof of their sincerity in trying to understand and respect other religions. It is dedicated to non-converting and most importantly improving relationships between faiths.

We also attend the annual interfaith holy day of peace among the religions of the world. It was last held at Christ Church Cranbrook (Episcopal), in Bloomfield Hills, Michigan. It is called the World Sabbath of Religious Reconciliation.

One more reference to religious pluralism. The Rabbi A James Ruden, uses an analogy to compare pluralism to a symphony orchestra with individual members or groups playing different instruments. By themselves they are only soloists, but playing together they make beautiful music. This implies that no one individual or group is more dominant than any of the other members. I might add that it relates to each of us perfecting our own faith or religion, but living with and respecting your neighbor's faith. In this way we can enjoy a moral and respectful community.

David Crumm, Free Press religion writer reporting on the November 1999 meeting of the National Council of Churches of Christ in the US makes it clear that current trends in free thinking are diversifying traditional church loyalties. This trend is increasing with larger numbers in the US involved in religion, spiritual concepts and religious books. Today every member of a family may belong to a different church.

Another Detroit Free Press report covered the new program at William Beaumont Hospital in Royal Oak, Michigan, which will consist of a planned Meditation Garden. This is the result of a survey confirming that recovery and even survival is linked to religious faith. There is a link between spiritual well being and healing. The hospital plans to cater to all faiths including Orthodox Jews, Muslims, East Indians, Asians, etc., by providing an area where incense can be burned and other required elements of the various religious rituals are available. The hospital chaplain staff and the nursing staff will have mandatory training in this area. This is another example of accepting and understanding religious diversity.

Considering the Ten Commandments and the rules and regulations of the many religions of the world, the contents and the requirements are almost identical. If everyone followed these rules perhaps the world's discords and disagreements would disappear and we could all live in peace and friendship

The one thing that stands out as a bright beacon in the darkness is that Jesus, Yahweh, Allah, Buddha, Confucius, Lao Tzo or Zoroaster, would all tell us to love and respect thy neighbor. We have not attained that goal, but history continues and hopefully one day love and respect will be a reality when we can accept and understand a neighbor's religion and thereby develop tolerance and achieve pluralism.

APPENDIX

World Religion Tree

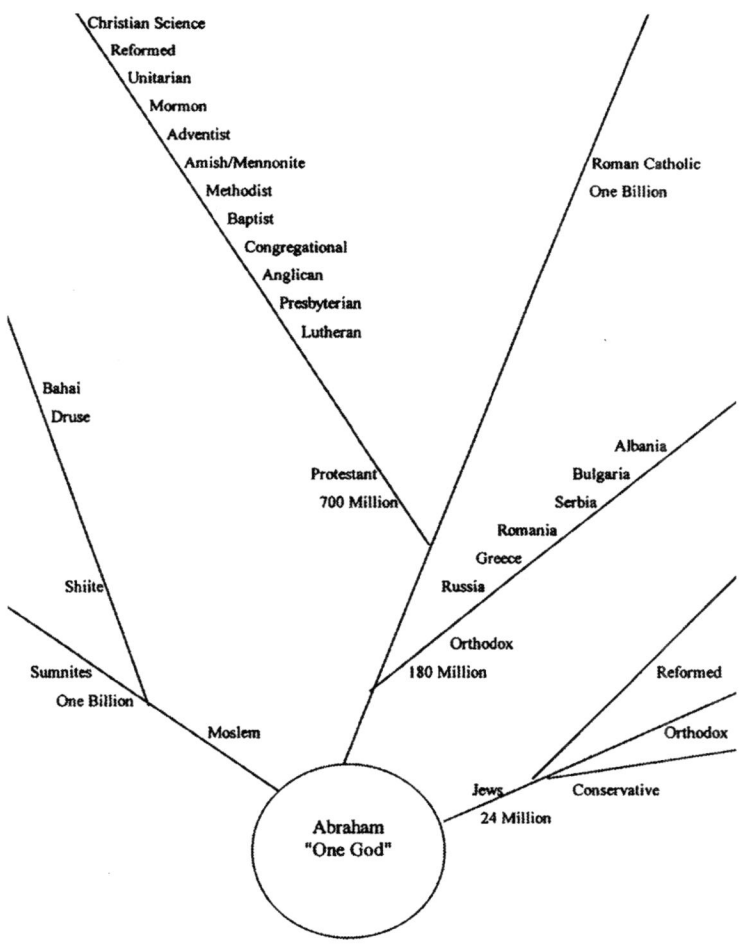

Bibliography

Adams, James L. Yankee Doodle Went To Church. New Jersey: Fleming H. Revell, 1970.

Angha, Molana Salaheddin Ali Nader Shah, Sufism The Reality of Religion. District of Columbia: MTO, 1998.

Armstrong, Karen. A History Of God. New York: Ballantine Books, 1993.

Basham, A.L. Classical Hinduism. New York: Oxford Press, 1989.

Bentley, James. Secrets of Mount Sinai. New York: Doubleday, 1986.

Bercot, David W. Real Heretics. Texas: Scroll, 1993.

Billings, Malcolm. The Crusades. New York: Sterling Publishing, 1996.

Borg, Marcus. Jesus and Buddha. Berkeley: Ulysses Press, 1997.

Brosse, Jacques. Religious Leaders. New York: Chambers, 1991.

Concordia Publishing. Comprehensive Bible History. Concordia: 1918.
(This is my original history book from grade school in 1929 at Emmanuel Lutheran School, Danville Illinois.)

Douglas, Elwell and Toon. Dictionary of Christian Tradition. Regency: 1989.

Dumoulin, Heinrich. Zen Buddhism. Prentice Hall Macmillan, 1988

Friedman, Richard Elliott. Who wrote the Bible? SanFrancisco: Harper, 1997.

Goring, Rosemary. Beliefs and Religions. New York: Larousse, 1994.

Halley, H.H. Bible Handbook. Grand Rapids: Zondervan Publishing, 1962.

Harper Collins. Atlas of the Bible. London: Harper Collins, 1987.

Hillerbrand, Hans J. The Protestant Reformation. New York: Harper and Row, 1968.

Jaspers, Karl. Socrates, Buddha, Confucius, Jesus. New York: Harvest Book, 1957.

Johnson, Paul G. God and World Religions. Pennsylvania: Ragged Edge Press, 1997.

Kennedy, Robert E. Zen Spirit, Christian Spirit. New York: Continuum, 1999.

Lapidoth, Ruth. Freedom of Religion in Jerusalem. Israel: The Jerusalem Institute of Israel Studies, 1999.

Lippman. Understanding Islam. New York: Penguin Books, 1995.

McEvedy, Colin. The New Penguin Atlas of Medieval History. New York: Penguin.

Miller, Madeleine. Harpers Bible Dictionary. New York: Harper, 1959

O'Grady, Joan. Early Christian Heresies. New York: Barnes and Noble Books, 1985.

Schaeffer, Frank. Dancing Alone. Brookline: Holy Cross Orthodox Press, 1994.

Snelling, John. <u>Buddhism</u>. Great Britain: Element Books, 1990.

Spong, John Shelby. <u>Why Christianity Must Change or Die.</u> San Francisco: Harper, 1998

Strathern, Paul. <u>Confucius in 90 Minutes</u>. Illinois: Ivan Dee, 1999.

Index

A
Adventist 113, 134
Alexander the Great 14, 15, 19
American Indian 131, 153
Amish 31, 32, 64, 97, 102, 151
Assembly of God 108, 122

B
Baha'i 141, 156, 160
Baptist 8, 18, 20, 21, 23, 25, 31, 96, 111, 112, 113, 124, 126, 127, 128, 145, 156, 157
Black Christians 128
Buddhism 3, 4, 20, 45, 46, 48, 50, 57, 75, 146, 147, 148, 149, 165, 167

C
Chaldeans 118
Charlemagne 41, 59, 61, 62
Christian Science 133, 156
Church of England 93, 94, 95, 104, 105, 111, 121, 131, 157
Church of God 122, 134
Church of Nazarene 122
Confucianism 4, 20, 57, 75
Congregational 53, 100, 101, 102, 109, 113, 124, 125, 157
Crusades 7, 67, 70, 71, 72, 165
Cults 129, 154

D
Deism 114, 115
Didache 28, 35
Disciples 18, 22, 25, 27, 124

E
Early Christians 21
Episcopal 41, 93, 94, 95, 96, 106, 107, 121, 126, 128, 131, 156, 157, 160

Essens 16, 18, 20

H
Hinduism 2, 3, 45, 57, 64, 141, 142, 149, 165
Holiness Movement 104, 122
Huguenot 92, 105

I
Inquisition 74, 75, 112
Islam 7, 34, 44, 48, 51, 52, 53, 54, 55, 56, 62, 63, 130, 135, 136, 137, 138, 139, 142, 144, 159, 166

J
Jains 45, 46, 142
Jehovah's Witness 133
Jesuits 90, 105, 117, 153, 156
John the Baptist 18, 20, 21, 23, 25, 31
Judaism 8, 16, 17, 33, 46, 143, 144, 145, 156

K
Krishna 58, 141

L
Lutheranism 91

M
Mennonites 97, 102, 151
Methodist 8, 96, 104, 111, 112, 121, 124, 128, 151, 156, 157
Mormons 131, 132
Music 5, 82, 95, 108, 109, 129, 137, 140, 151, 160

N
Nation of Islam 129

New Testament 25, 26, 27, 31, 33, 35, 48, 49, 77, 79, 85, 87, 88, 89, 93, 133

O

Orthodox Catholic 37, 63, 91

P

Pentecostal 122, 133
Philosophers 11, 16
Pietism 91, 125, 150
Pilgrims 99, 100, 101, 124
Presbyterian 82, 90, 93, 111, 113, 124, 128, 130, 156, 157
Puritans 82, 97, 98, 99, 101, 111, 114, 122, 126

R

Reformed 82, 90, 124, 125, 130, 144, 157
Roman Catholic 37, 48, 62, 63, 79, 84, 90, 92, 93, 95, 96, 98, 104, 105, 114, 116, 118, 120, 154, 159

S

Salvation Army 151

Scientist 11, 15, 83, 133
Scientology 152
Separatist 96
Septuagint 15, 19, 88
Seventh Day Adventist 113, 133, 134
Shakers 134
Sikhism 141, 142
Southern Baptist 127, 156, 157
St. Augustine 5, 42, 45, 53, 87, 94, 104, 152

T

Taoism 4, 5, 11
Twelve Tribes 12, 16

U

Unitarians 123

V

Vulgate 28, 48, 77, 88, 115

Z

Zoroastrianism 5, 19, 34

0-595-23062-8